St Davids Bishop's Palace
St Non's Chapel

The Rt Revd J. Wyn Evans BA, BD, FSA, FRHistS, Bishop of St Davids
and Rick Turner MA, FSA

A Palace for Prelates 3

A History of the Palace 5
Beginnings 5
The Norman Centuries 7
The Thirteenth and Fourteenth Centuries 10
The Later Middle Ages 20
Reformation and Decline 22

A Tour of the Palace 27
The Plan and Construction of the Palace 27
The East Range 28
The South Range 37
The West Range 44
The Undercrofts 44
The Exterior of the Palace 47

St Non's Chapel 51

Features
The Wealth and Power of the Bishops of St Davids 12
Bishop Henry de Gower: Architectural Patron 18
Recent Conservation at the Palace 35
Sculpted Decoration and the Arcaded Parapet 42
The Cathedral Close 48

Further Reading 52

A Palace for Prelates

Hic iacet Henricus Gower quondam Menevensis Episcopus et Episcopalis Palacii constructor ...

Here lies Henry Gower, some time Bishop of St Davids and builder of the Episcopal Palace ...

Thus, according to the account of the eighteenth-century antiquary, Edward Yardley, ran the epitaph of Henry de Gower, bishop of St Davids from 1328 to 1347. It was once affixed to the metal railing around his tomb in the great stone pulpitum which he caused to be built under the west crossing arch in the cathedral church. It could equally well have described him as 'beautifier of his cathedral, academic, and servant of the Crown'. Instead, it was as the builder of the palace that he was remembered at St Davids — long after the destruction of his epitaph and the railings to which it was attached, long indeed after the palace itself had fallen into ruin.

Not, however, that the epitaph was entirely true. There were at least some portions of the present palace structure in existence before Bishop Henry's time, and other hands modified the buildings a little after his day. It was he, none the less, who appears to have commissioned an entire rebuilding of the palace, bringing it in several phases to a state of near harmonious perfection. Moreover, although there were other episcopal residences in the vast medieval diocese of St Davids, some of which also benefited from Henry de Gower's architectural attentions, it was the one at St Davids which was always referred to as *Palatium*, the palace par excellence. It was Gower who is rightly identified as its greatest and most celebrated champion.

Above: The seal of Henry de Gower, bishop of St Davids from 1328 to 1347 (The Society of Antiquaries of London).

Left: Henry de Gower's tomb lies at the southern end of the richly ornamented pulpitum screen that he erected in St Davids Cathedral. The metal railing around the tomb and the epitaph, which commemorated Gower as 'the builder of the Episcopal Palace', had already disappeared when John Buckler (d. 1851) made this drawing in 1815 (© The British Library Board, Additional Ms. 36397, f. 61).

Opposite: The bishop's palace and cathedral reflect the architectural ambitions of numerous bishops of the diocese. It is, however, Bishop Gower who is remembered as the principal architect of the palace, responsible for much of what is visible today, including the magnificent great hall.

Memoria de sancto david
confessor. Antiphona

ste est qui ante
deum magnas
virtutes opa-
tus est et omis

A History of the Palace

Beginnings

The story of St Davids, whether it be that of the palace, the cathedral or the diocese, begins long before the time of Henry de Gower. This spot on the banks of the river Alun, where it passes into a deep, sheltered but marshy valley a mile (1.6km) or so above its entry into the sea at Porth Clais, is generally believed to be the *Vallis Rosina* — the 'valley of the little marsh' — chosen some time during the sixth century as the site of his monastic foundation by David, the patron saint of Wales. There are, however, other claimants for that original site: Tygwyn, at nearby Whitesands Bay, and Henfynyw (Old Menevia), near Aberaeron. David's monastery, known as *Mynyw* (Latin *Menevia*), a word derived from, or cognate with, the Irish word *muine* meaning a 'bush' or a 'brake', gave the name in the medieval period both to the cathedral and to the diocese.

The site became famous, not only for an ascetic monasticism, but also for learning. David's asceticism, as described by the eleventh-century scholar-cleric Rhigyfarch (d. 1099), meant that he and his community lived their ordered life of prayer, dressed in animal skins, existing on the bare necessities of life, and drawing the plough themselves as they tilled their fields. It was the asceticism of *Menevia* which drew the attention of Irish monks of the eighth century as they embarked on the monastic reform. It also guaranteed the wealth and privileges of the site, as grateful pilgrims and others made gifts of land and food renders to the church. Such wealth, however, attracted less welcome visitors, culminating in a series of attacks by the Vikings in the tenth and eleventh centuries. At least two bishops were killed — one of whom is known to have been Morgeneu, who died in a raid in 999. His death was traditionally ascribed to his being the first bishop to abandon the ascetic tradition of the saint himself by eating meat.

The tradition of learning meant that, from at least the eighth century, a chronicle was kept at St Davids; it is from this source that we learn of the depredations of the Vikings. It was the same tradition which also caused Asser to be called from St Davids by King Alfred at the end of the ninth century, to aid in the restoration of civilized life in Wessex following the damage done by the Danes. Further, for two periods of five years in the eleventh century (1073–78 and 1080–85), St Davids was the seat of Bishop Sulien, one of the most distinguished Welsh scholars of the pre-Conquest period. His sons, the eldest of whom was Rhigyfarch — writer of the earliest surviving life (*vita*) of David — did much to foster the intellectual life of their day. It was Sulien, in company with Rhys ap Tewdwr,

Opposite: St David, the patron saint of Wales, shown here in a fifteenth-century manuscript illumination in the Hastings Hours *(© The British Library Board, Additional Ms. 54782, f. 40).*

*Below: David's asceticism was described by the scholar-cleric, Rhigyfarch (d. 1099), in his life (*vita*) of the saint. This copy was probably written in Gloucester around 1200 (© The British Library Board, Cotton Vespasian Ms. A XIV, f. 61).*

HISTORY: BEGINNINGS

Above: The cathedral church at St Davids and the bishop's palace beyond lie in the sheltered valley of the river Alun. Tradition associates this site with that chosen by David for his monastic foundation sometime during the sixth century.

Right: St David's relics were treasured possessions of the cathedral and attracted pilgrims throughout the Middle Ages, including a visit by William I in 1081. In 1275, a new shrine for the relics was created on the north side of the presbytery near the high altar, and its base, shown here, still survives (Dean and Chapter of St Davids Cathedral).

1093), the king of south Wales who had found *nawdd* (refuge) at St Davids, who went down to Porth Clais to meet Gruffudd ap Cynan (d. 1137), king of Gwynedd, returning from Ireland. In the presence of Bishop Sulien, the two kings made a compact in the cathedral over the relics of St David before they proceeded to victory over their common enemy at Mynydd Carn in 1081. It was such involvement in politics on the part of St Davids and its bishops which no doubt attracted the attention of William the Conqueror and brought him there in the year of Mynydd Carn. This visit, ostensibly for prayer, was a harbinger of the changes which would affect both the cathedral and the diocese.

In the case of both the cathedral and the palace, very few archaeological remains survive from the period prior to the establishment of the first Norman bishop. There are, none the less, some carved gravestones and crosses from the close and the cathedral. They range from simple water-worn boulders, inscribed with a cross and sacred monogram, to a portion of a highly decorated standing cross.

HISTORY: THE NORMAN CENTURIES

In addition, from the site of the palace, and discovered during the clearance operations in the central courtyard in 1937, are two silver coins. The one is a penny of King Harold II who fell at Hastings; it is dated to 1066. The other is a penny of William I (1066–87) and dates from around 1086.

Of interest in this connection is the existence of silver coinage struck for William at a mint known as DEVITUN. Given that the episcopal mill below the earth castle is still known as Dewiston, it has been suggested that the mint was at St Davids. Archaeological excavations on the site of the ticket office at the palace in 1973 revealed not only traces of a bank along the line of the later enclosure wall, but also a piece of Anglo-Norman pottery. There was thus activity on the site of the present building in the eleventh century, but it is impossible to determine its nature. Nor is it possible to locate the episcopal residence of the period with any certainty.

Given the repeated destruction of St Davids during the eleventh and preceding centuries, it is not surprising that no traces survive of either the pre-Conquest cathedral or of its attendant domestic structures. Indeed, the life of St Caradog, a monk who lived in the late eleventh and early twelfth centuries, suggests that at that time the site was not only deserted, but overgrown to the extent that the tomb of the patron saint himself was almost inaccessible behind a screen of bushes and brambles. This may have been the result of the raid by the 'Norsemen of the Isles' in 1091.

The Norman Centuries

In 1115, Bernard — chaplain to Henry I's queen, Matilda (d. 1118) — became the first Norman bishop of the diocese (1115–48). Given the size and wealth of this, the largest diocese in Wales, and its strategic importance in relation to Ireland, as demonstrated by Gruffudd ap Cynan's landing, it is not surprising that the Crown should have wished to see a Norman rather than a native Welshman as bishop of *Menevia*. On the other hand, Bernard proved himself not only an effective reformer of both cathedral and diocese, but also maintained and defended the ancient privileges of *Menevia*, including its persistent claim to have been a metropolitan or archiepiscopal see.

Above: The reverse of a silver penny of William the Conqueror (1066–87), struck at a mint known as DEVITUN. *It has been suggested that this mint was located at St Davids (National Museum of Wales).*

Above left: Few remains survive at St Davids that can be dated to before the arrival of the first Norman bishop in 1115. This early Christian cross, however, dates from about 1070–80 and commemorates the two sons of Bishop Abraham. Originally erected as a free-standing monument, it was later built into the east wall of the south transept of the cathedral, and is now displayed in the Porth y Tŵr.

Although the first Norman bishop, Bernard, was appointed in 1115, few representations of the early Norman and English bishops survive. However, this very fine tomb in the south choir of the cathedral is that of Bishop Anselm le Gras (1231–47) (Dean and Chapter of St Davids Cathedral).

The accession of Bishop Bernard and his medieval successors brings us to the development of the cathedral, palace and the surrounding close as we see them today. Nothing now survives of the cathedral church which Bernard is known to have raised in 1131, with the possible exception of some carved stonework reused in the tower. Nor is there evidence of an episcopal residence for the very earliest Norman bishops, though it has been suggested that this function was served by a small earthwork castle above the valley to the west of the close.

Again, while it is clear that the cathedral was extensively reconstructed in the later twelfth century, there is exceedingly little evidence either for the location or the nature of the episcopal residence. The version of the Latin chronicle kept at *Menevia*, in its obituary notice of Peter de Leia, bishop in 1176–98, tells us that it was he who began the 'new work' which is represented by the greater part of the present cathedral, in particular the nave arcades.

However, in the account given by the Welsh chronicle — *Brut y Tywysogyon* — of the pilgrimage to *Menevia* by King Henry II (1154–89) in September 1171, we are told that the bishop, David fitz Gerald (1148–76), invited the English monarch to dine with him at his *llys* (court). King Henry felt that this would entail excessive expense for the bishop but was nevertheless prevailed upon to dine, and entered the *neuadd* (hall), together with the bishop and three canons. Unfortunately, the exact location of this building is unknown.

On his return from Ireland on Easter Monday 1172, Henry made a second pilgrimage to the cathedral. This was the occasion when, after being met at the White Gate by the canons, he crossed the Llech Lafar (Talking Stone) which bridged the river Alun near the north-west corner of the cathedral. On this occasion, too, he dined at St Davids, but again at an unknown location. Later in the same century, when Gerald of Wales (d. 1223) — in company with Baldwin, archbishop of Canterbury (1184–90) — came here on his journey through Wales in 1188, he recorded that they were given good accommodation by Bishop Peter de Leia. Whether this was in the bishop's own residence or elsewhere is not made clear.

The western range of the palace may date from the end of the twelfth or early years of the thirteenth century, but the lack of any detailed features makes it impossible to be certain.

Opposite: The richly decorated nave in the cathedral at St Davids was begun in the 1180s, during the time of Bishop Peter de Leia (1176–98). Although the cathedral was undergoing a major programme of reconstruction, there is very little evidence for the state of the palace buildings at this time (Dean and Chapter of St Davids Cathedral).

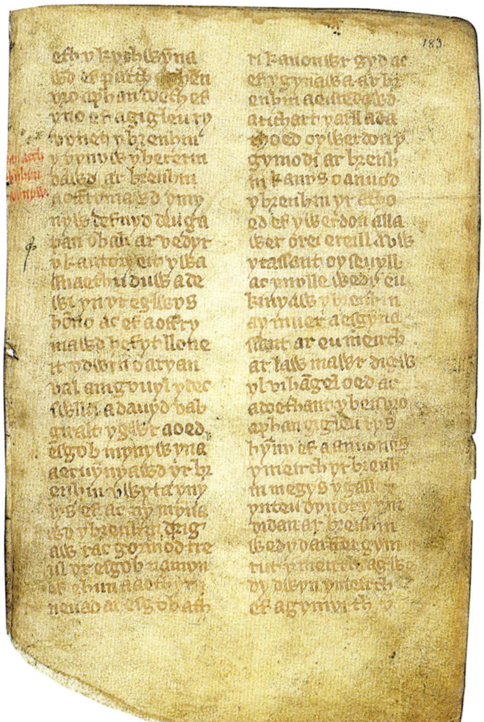

*Far left: King Henry II (1154–89) twice visited St Davids — on pilgrimage in September 1171 and again on his return from Ireland on Easter Monday 1172. This page from the Welsh Chronicle of the Princes (*Brut y Tywysogyon*) records the earlier visit when Bishop David fitz Gerald invited the king to dine with him at his court (*llys*) (National Library of Wales, Peniarth Ms. 20, p. 183).*

Left: Henry II — shown here in a near contemporary manuscript illustration from Gerald of Wales's Conquest of Ireland *— dined with fitz Gerald for a second time on his 1172 visit to the cathedral (National Library of Ireland, Ms. 700).*

The Thirteenth and Fourteenth Centuries

During the thirteenth and fourteenth centuries the bishops appointed to the diocese of *Menevia* had already been — and in some cases continued to be — royal civil servants or chancellors of the university of Oxford. Such were Thomas Bek, bishop from 1280 until 1293 (chancellor of the university of Oxford and keeper of the king's wardrobe); David Martin, 1293–1327 (chancellor of the university of Oxford); Henry de Gower, 1328–47 (chancellor of the university of Oxford); John Thoresby, 1347–49 (lord chancellor of England); and Adam de Houghton, 1362–89 (lord treasurer of England). Many of these, together with less distinguished bishops of *Menevia*, were born in Wales, among them Gower, Martin and Houghton.

Bishop Thomas Bek (1280–93)

Thomas Bek was born of a Lincolnshire family which for more than a century had served kings, earls and bishops, and had risen by means of this service to the ranks of minor nobility. His younger brother, Anthony, was to become one of the three great councillors of King Edward I (1272–1307), and in 1284 was awarded a prestigious and powerful appointment as bishop of Durham (1284–1311). Indeed, it was Anthony, already at the court of the recently crowned king, who probably secured for Thomas the office as keeper of the wardrobe in 1274.

Thomas began his career at Oxford where he became a master of arts and, by 1269, chancellor of the university. He succeeded Anthony as keeper of the wardrobe and served Edward I loyally in this responsible office, particularly during the king's first Welsh war of 1276–77. His election to the bishopric of St Davids was undoubtedly a preferment for his reliable support and administration. By the same token, the king was clearly seeking to place a man that he could trust in this position of considerable authority. In short, by the time of his arrival at St Davids, Bek was already a man rich in the experience of the affairs of state. Now he was to become something of a champion of his see, a benefactor and reformer, and a builder of some note.

It seems, for example, that the detached bell tower — against which Porth y Tŵr (Tower Gate) was later built — was erected about this time. The visit of King Edward I and Queen Eleanor to St Davids in 1284 may have influenced some reconstruction, and it is known that the king made

Above: The seal of Bishop Thomas Bek (1280–93), on which he is depicted in eucharistic vestments, holding his pastoral staff in his left hand (The Society of Antiquaries of London).

Right: This late thirteenth-century manuscript illustration shows bishops in attendance on King Edward I (1272–1307). The preferment of royal civil servants to the diocese of Menevia helped to ensure loyalty to the Crown, and in this King Edward's appointment of Bishop Thomas Bek — his former keeper of the wardrobe — was no exception (© The British Library Board, Cotton Vitellius Ms. A XIII, f. 6v).

Far right: The detached bell tower, to the left of Porth y Tŵr (one of the four gates into the cathedral close), appears to have been built towards the end of the thirteenth century, and may be the work of Bishop Bek.

a gift towards the works which he had requested Bek to undertake at the cathedral.

The cathedral close seems also to have benefited from Bek's attentions (pp. 48–49). He reorganized the cathedral chapter, and in 1287 he ordered the canons to enclose their houses. This may mean that he was ordering the enclosure of each individual property, or it may refer to the construction of the wall encircling the close — or the city — of St Davids. That such a close existed prior to 1326 is revealed in the *Black Book* (p. 12) which mentions the pasture within the walls. There was clearly some kind of enclosure here before this date, for in 1172 the canons met Henry II at the 'White Gate'. Given the importance of St Davids as a centre of pilgrimage and place of sanctuary, it is very likely that some kind of boundary had been erected even earlier than this — not only to define the sacred enclosure, but also to defend the cathedral and episcopal and prebendal houses. Yet, since no building accounts survive, it is impossible to date the construction of the close wall. Indeed, it is the detached bell tower next to Porth y Tŵr which is the datable architectural feature associated with the wall, and this is considered to have been erected towards the end of the thirteenth century.

Thomas Bek was also aware of the earlier pretensions of St Davids as a metropolitan see, since he attempted to defend them at the visitation which Archbishop John Pecham (1279–92) held at St Davids in July 1284. In this, however, he proved unsuccessful. Even so, Bek achieved much in the diocese during his episcopate. In one remarkable year (1287), he founded hospitals at Llawhaden and St Davids, a collegiate church at Llanddewi Brefi, and re-established a second college at Abergwili near Carmarthen.

Bishop Bek seems to have expended some effort on the buildings of the cathedral close. The extent of his work is not clear, though it was certainly not long after Bek's episcopate that the close was brought to the form it was to retain until well into the eighteenth century. In 1720, this plan of the close was made by Joseph Lord for Bishop Adam Ottley (1713–23) (see p. 25). Although the houses of the dean and chapter have since been rebuilt or fallen into ruin, much of the basic detail can still be seen today (National Library of Wales, SD/CH/B 29).

The Wealth and Power of the Bishops of St Davids

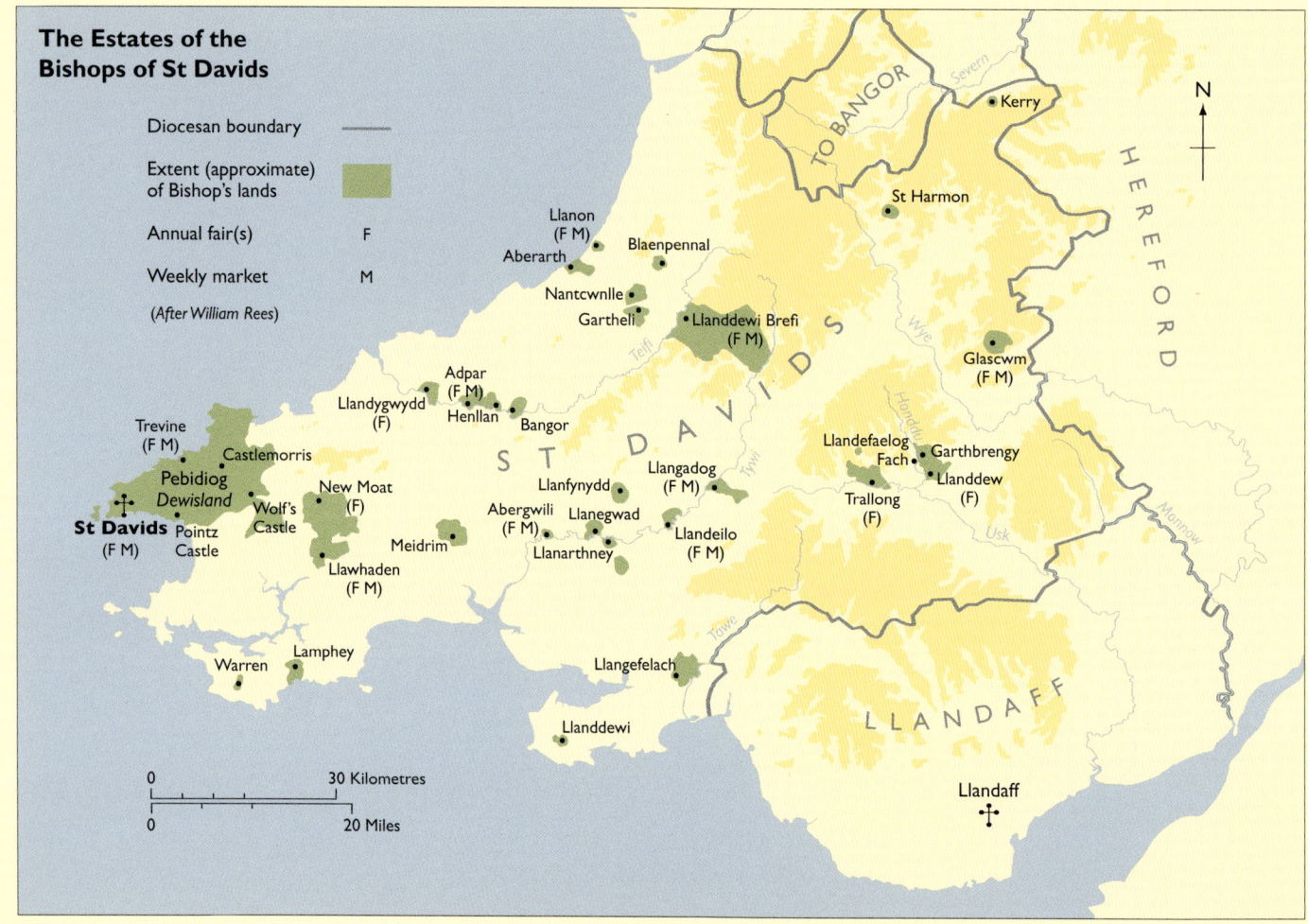

That men such as Thomas Bek, David Martin, Henry de Gower and Adam de Houghton were rewarded with the see of St Davids should cause no surprise. The largest diocese in medieval Wales, it was also the richest. The great record made for David Martin in 1326, and known as the *Black Book of St Davids*, reveals that the diocesan estates rendered a profit of £333 to the bishop in that year.

The bishop's demesne lands were found in several compact blocks in the wealthiest parts of the diocese, for example in the Tywi and Teifi valleys and around Brecon. Dewisland, the Welsh *cantref* of Pebidiog, the area around St Davids itself, was believed to have been bestowed upon the bishops by the largesse of the royal house of Deheubarth. The prince to whom this gift was attributed was Rhys ap Tewdwr, who died in battle with the Normans in 1093. Indeed it may have been granted in gratitude for the *nawdd* (refuge or sanctuary) he enjoyed here in 1081. Further, it is clear that the area was wealthy in pre-Norman times, as witnessed by the frequent Viking raids on St Davids. No doubt it was the popularity of the church of David as a pilgrimage centre which ensured the continuing wealth of St Davids throughout the medieval period; and which found practical expression in the quality of the architecture still to be seen in both cathedral and palace.

In the time of Bishop Bernard (1115–48), papal privileges were secured for the site so that in time it came to be believed that two pilgrimages to St Davids were equal to one to Rome. This was expressed in the Latin rhyme: *Roma semel quantum bis dat Menevia tantum*.

With the landed possessions and wealth of the see went great temporal power. The bishop of St Davids was a Lord Marcher, holding his lordship directly from the Crown, with royal jurisdiction in all his lordships. These regalian rights, safeguarded and confirmed by successive royal charters, included a prison, gallows, and the right to hold courts. The tenants of the episcopal estates in what is now Pembrokeshire had to follow the bishop with the shrine of St Davids and the relics in time of war. He received the income from the tolls at those fairs and markets which King Edward I granted in 1281 to Bishop Bek at St Davids and Llawhaden. The bishop had a castle at Llawhaden which served as the administrative centre of his estates. In the places where the right to hold markets had been secured, boroughs were founded: that at St Davids was centred around the market cross on the higher ground to the south-west of the cathedral.

It was this wealth and status, further secured by the more settled conditions obtaining in the Wales of the post-Edwardian conquest, which were reflected in the architecture of the fourteenth-century palace.

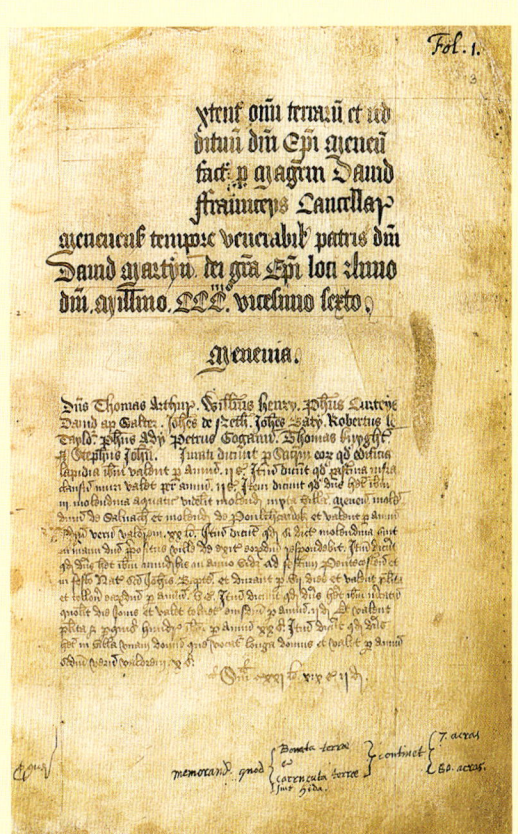

Above: During the Middle Ages, the bishops of St Davids wielded great temporal as well as spiritual power. In time of war, the tenants of the episcopal estates had to follow the bishop with the shrine and relics of St David. This mid-thirteenth-century manuscript illustration shows a bishop clad for war (© The British Library Board, Cotton Nero Ms. D II, f. 121v).

Above left: The Black Book of St Davids *was compiled in 1326 for Bishop David Martin (1293–1327) by the chancellor, David Francis. A detailed survey of all the lands and estates held by the bishop, it was kept for centuries as a source of reference. This surviving copy dates from the early sixteenth century, when it was renewed for Bishop Edward Vaughan (1509–22) (© The British Library Board, Additional Ms. 34135, f. 3).*

Left: Llawhaden Castle served as the administrative centre of one of the more profitable estates of the bishops of St Davids. In 1281, King Edward I granted Bishop Thomas Bek the right to hold a weekly market there, plus two annual three-day fairs, the tolls for which continued to increase the wealth of the bishops of St Davids (Skyscan Balloon Photography for Cadw).

HISTORY: THE THIRTEENTH AND FOURTEENTH CENTURIES

Bishop Henry de Gower — the greatest of the medieval bishops of St Davids — was buried in a splendid tomb in the cathedral, when he died in April 1347. Bishop Henry had chosen the spot before his death, on the south side of the pulpitum screen that he erected at the east end of the nave. Despite mutilation, Gower's effigy on the tomb lid remains an impressive reminder of this remarkable builder-bishop (Dean and Chapter of St Davids Cathedral).

Bishop Henry de Gower (1328–47)

Following the death of Bishop David Martin in 1327, a full survey of the St Davids episcopal estates was undertaken. Puzzling, perhaps, is the reference to St Davids itself, where it is stated 'there is a *mansio* for servants and animals in winter, where there ought to be a palace, worth 6*d.* per annum'.

In short, regardless of the domestic residences of his predecessors, when Henry de Gower was elected to the see at St Davids he appears to have inherited a largely empty precinct. Thereafter, it was Gower who raised the palace which continues to grace the cathedral city. The work appears to have been completed in several stages, but with his masons following a single harmonious scheme.

Henry de Gower was born in about 1278 and was probably of noble birth. He very likely came from the area of the Gower peninsula in south Wales. The latter suggestion is borne out by the fact that he founded a hospital in Swansea; and he may well have influenced some rebuilding at Swansea Castle, where an arcaded parapet similar to that at St Davids was added in the second quarter of the fourteenth century.

Bishop Henry was a graduate of Merton College, Oxford and by 1320 had taken the degree of doctor of civil law; by 1322 he was a doctor of canon law. From 1322 until 1325 he was the chancellor of the university. About 1314 he became a canon of St Davids, and then successively archdeacon (by 1326) and eventually bishop in 1328. Although, unlike other medieval bishops of St Davids, he had never been a full-time civil servant, he had nevertheless served the Crown in various capacities during the reign of King

HISTORY: THE THIRTEENTH AND FOURTEENTH CENTURIES

Edward III (1327–77), and received many privileges from that monarch.

The surviving capitular and episcopal documents show him to have been an active bishop, concerned to reform both the administration of the diocese and the lives of the clergy. His abiding achievement remains visible in the building work he undertook both in the episcopal residences and in the cathedral. Clearly, he had the financial and artistic resources at his disposal to construct big, bold and highly decorated buildings of fine quality.

In addition to his work at the palace, there is in the statute book of the cathedral an ordinance of Bishop Gower, dated 27 May 1342, which lists the buildings on the various episcopal manors which were to be kept in repair. It is clear that many of the buildings were uninhabitable. Those that were ruinous were to be demolished and their materials used for the repair of the others. Seven were to be retained for the benefit of the bishop and his successors. The palace at St Davids heads the list. Whether this was an attempt at retrenchment following expenditure on the palace, or part of a general refurbishment of which the work at St Davids was a part, is now impossible to determine.

Henry de Gower also paid some attention to the close, and to the canons' houses. Within the context of enforcing residence by the canons and the consequent provision by each canon of a house fit for him to live in, he referred — in an ordinance dated 28 June 1344 — to 'the new close' (pp. 48–49). Perhaps, then, the close wall and gateways were refurbished — if not constructed — during his episcopate; or possibly the close may just have been enlarged by him. Bishop Fastolfe (1353–61) certainly believed that Gower had built the close: in a document of 1358 he mentioned the *clausum honestum* which Henry, 'one of his predecessors' as bishop, had made. He gave a curious reason for this work by Gower. It was said to safeguard the canons, vicars, and ministers of the cathedral from the depredations of the bishop's temporal officers. Interestingly, the upper chamber of Porth y Tŵr was crowned with a battlement which is similar to that on the great chapel of the palace.

Overall, Bishop Henry's extraordinarily ambitious programme of works at the palace resulted in a handsome new arrangement, with a double set of spacious apartments on two sides of the courtyard (pp. 27–28). The range on the eastern side appears to

Far left: Henry de Gower's architectural aspirations — as well as his concerns for the poor and sick clergy of the diocese — found some expression in Swansea. Here, in 1332, he founded the hospital of the Blessed St David, fragments of which survive in the Cross Keys Inn. Gower's association with the chief town in the lordship of Gower may reflect the bishop's origins in this area of south Wales.

Left: Bishop Henry's association with Swansea may have influenced the design of the new lodgings wing added to Swansea Castle in the second quarter of the fourteenth century. Although the parapet bears a close resemblance to Gower's work at St Davids, there is no evidence to indicate that the bishop was directly involved in its construction.

HISTORY: THE THIRTEENTH AND FOURTEENTH CENTURIES

HISTORY: THE THIRTEENTH AND FOURTEENTH CENTURIES

have been planned as private accommodation, essentially for the use of the bishop himself. These rooms were complemented by an even grander block of apartments — focusing on a great hall — forming the south wing of the quadrangle.

This double arrangement can also be seen at a number of other episcopal palaces in Britain, such as Lincoln, Wells and Wolvesey. Whereas the one range would have been used by the bishops as their lodgings when they visited their cathedral, the other would have been used for the entertainment of distinguished guests or on state occasions. The great hall may also have been used as a hall of audience, and, perhaps, for the administration of justice, since the bishop of St Davids was, as a Lord Marcher, a great temporal lord, whose tenants had to appear in the episcopal courts. While there is no direct evidence that such activity took place at St Davids, unlike at Castle Maurice or later at Llawhaden, it is inherently likely that the great hall provided a seemly setting for the episcopal court.

Bishop Adam de Houghton (1362–89)

It has been suggested that work on the palace continued after Gower's day into the episcopate of Adam de Houghton (1362–89). Bishop Adam certainly undertook building work, adding the college and chantry chapel of the Blessed Virgin Mary, with its attendant cloister on the north side of the cathedral. And it was Houghton who completely remodelled the bishop's castle at Llawhaden. All of these buildings, however, were built in the early Perpendicular style of Gothic architecture, in contrast to the Decorated style associated with Gower.

Adam de Houghton also re-enacted Gower's ordinances regarding the manorial and other episcopal buildings which were to be kept in repair. Of more interest is Houghton's order that each canon, 'for the good and security' of those who lived within the close, should contribute towards the repair of the gates and walls of the said close (pp. 48–49). Twenty shillings were demanded for the work. The reason given for this order was that the gates and walls were in ruins, and to a great extent 'consumed with age'. Such decay in gates and walls, only twenty years or so after Gower's death, seems surprising. It may thus be the case that Bishop Henry's work on the close was that of a major refurbishment rather than construction anew.

Above: The seal of Adam de Houghton, 1365, bishop of St Davids between 1362 and 1389. Above the bishop stand the figures of St David and St Andrew, the patrons of the cathedral (The National Archives: PRO, DL 27/102).

Left: By the mid-fourteenth century, the palace and cathedral close were at their zenith, as shown in this reconstruction drawing (Illustration by Terry Ball, 1989; with modifications, 1999).

Henry de Gower's handsome pulpitum screen in the cathedral church at St Davids. Designed and finely carved in the Decorated style, Gower planned the pulpitum to accommodate his own ornate tomb (Dean and Chapter of St Davids Cathedral).

Built in the last decade of the thirteenth century, the choir of the chapel at Merton College, Oxford is a fine example of a building in the Decorated style. Henry de Gower, who studied at the college and became a fellow there in 1307, would have been familiar with the chapel and its architectural details (Anthony Kersting).

Bishop Henry de Gower: Architectural Patron

Born about 1278, and bishop of St Davids from 1328 until 1347, Henry de Gower undoubtedly had a passion for architecture. During his nineteen years in episcopal office, he not only rebuilt the bishop's palace, but also remodelled the nave, choir and tower of the cathedral, beautified the Lady Chapel there, and erected the pulpitum screen which served as his burial place. Elsewhere he extended the palace at Lamphey, built a residence at Llanddewi in Gower, and may have influenced the new lodgings wing with its arcaded parapet at Swansea Castle. Finally, it was in Swansea, too, that he built a large hospital for the poor and sick clergy of the diocese. Bishop Henry achieved all this on an annual income of about £350, a sum which was rather less than that available to most other bishops, and only about one-eighth of the size of the two richest dioceses — Durham and Winchester. Moreover, it seems the bishop had little private wealth.

Having studied at Merton College, Oxford, Henry de Gower became a fellow there in 1307. Later, in 1322–25, he was chancellor of the university. At the time, Merton was not only a place of great scholarship, it was also a centre of architectural innovation with some of the finest new buildings in the Decorated style under construction. It appears Gower was also a friend of Abbot Edmund Knowle (1306–32), during whose time a marvellously original and inventive scheme of work was undertaken at St Augustine's Abbey, Bristol (now the cathedral). Both as chancellor and later as bishop, Henry de Gower would have had frequent cause to journey to London, attending court and parliament. Here he would have had the opportunity to observe and discuss the latest architectural trends emanating from the capital. At last, at the age of about fifty, his election to the see of St Davids allowed for the release of his architectural ambitions.

The contemporary style of Gothic architecture known as Decorated was to all intents and purposes restricted to England and Wales. In broad terms, it flourished between the mid-thirteenth and the mid-fourteenth centuries. It is suggested that the essence of the style was the 'illumination' of architectural spaces. This was achieved by the lavish application of ornament, including fine carving, flowing tracery and rich colour. As for earlier centuries, it is argued that we can identify distinct regional schools within the Decorated era, with one of the most important of these centred on the Severnside region. Major building schemes at, for example, the cathedrals of Exeter and Wells, and the abbeys at Bristol and Tintern were the product of the architectural lodges in this area.

We must remember that the profession of architect as it is known today did not appear until the seventeenth century. The design of great medieval buildings was the result of the interplay between educated patrons and their master craftsmen, adopting the conventions of the current style and using existing buildings as models.

Careful study of the architecture in the bishop's palace — including the moulded profiles of doorways and window jambs and the carved sculptural detail — suggests that two master masons and at least one master sculptor from the Bristol area were responsible for realizing Gower's ambitions at St Davids. They worked not only on the palace, but no doubt also on the contemporary work on the cathedral.

So it was that Henry de Gower came to build the bishop's palace, probably the most important secular building in the Decorated style to survive anywhere in England and Wales. It was probably the modest diocesan income which led to the use of local stone, with the walls raised in rubble and then covered in painted plaster. In fact, the Caerbwdi sandstone was the only local material which could be dressed and carved, and its purple colour was a bonus. Fine and expensively carved decoration was limited to where it would have the greatest impact: the two doorways into the bishop's hall, the great hall porch, and the east end and the interior of the great chapel. The greatest ornament, however, was reserved for the brilliantly innovative arcaded parapet (p. 42), though even here the full adornments were only applied to the most prominent elevations.

In all, Bishop Henry de Gower showed not only a genius for architectural design but also for the most effective use of his available resources.

Far left: The choir of St Augustine's Abbey, Bristol (now the cathedral) was rebuilt to an original and inventive design during the abbacy of Edmund Knowle (1306–32). Henry de Gower was a friend of Knowle and may have seen the new work at Bristol. Architectural details in the bishop's palace suggest that two master masons and at least one master sculptor from the Bristol area also worked at St Davids (Angelo Hornak Photograph Library, London).

Left: The 'illuminated' Decorated architecture of the nave of Exeter Cathedral, which was completed around the middle of the fourteenth century. Although the colours that would have enriched the scene in the Middle Ages have largely disappeared, the lavish architectural and sculptural ornamentation is still impressive (Angelo Hornak Photograph Library, London).

The Later Middle Ages

Below: Henry Chichele was one of the more distinguished later medieval bishops of St Davids (1408–14). He later became archbishop of Canterbury (1414–43), where he is buried in this magnificent tomb in the north choir aisle. His lavish effigy on the tomb lid contrasts with the corpse in the tomb chest — a common theme in the later Middle Ages (Topfoto/ Woodmansterne).

Below right: Robert Sherborne (1505–08) also became a bishop of some note, distinguishing himself as a patron of the arts when he moved to the diocese of Chichester. This painting of Bishop Robert, thought to date from around 1520, comes from a large wooden panel depicting the medieval bishops of Chichester in the north transept of the cathedral (Peter Humphries/Dean and Chapter of Chichester Cathedral).

From the end of Adam de Houghton's episcopate, right through to the time of Bishop Edward Vaughan (1509–22), by and large Henry de Gower's successors were men of lesser note — certainly in terms of building work at St Davids. Although there is evidence that some of these later bishops took an interest in other palaces within the diocese, there is very little to indicate significant building at St Davids after about 1350. This is not to say that some of the bishops of the later Middle Ages were not men of great interest. Henry Chichele (1408–14), for example, moved from St Davids to become archbishop of Canterbury (1414–43), whereas Bishop Robert Sherborne (1505–08) was translated to the diocese of Chichester, where he became a distinguished patron of the arts involved in a number of building and decorative schemes at various episcopal residences.

Here at St Davids, however, the veil on later medieval episcopal life at the palace is lifted briefly in the account of the enthronement of Bishop Guy de Mone (1397–1407). On 8 September 1398, the bishop walked barefoot from Capel y Gwrhyd (Fathom Chapel), which lay just outside the great linear earthwork known today as Ffos y Mynach that probably marked the limit of sanctuary around the cathedral. Having covered the mile and a half (2.4km) to St Davids in this painful fashion, he was met at the city (the cathedral close), by the cathedral canons and the people and clergy of the diocese. He was then conducted to the high altar of the cathedral and afterwards enthroned. After celebrating Mass, he then proceeded to the palace, where he kept 'for some time the festival customary on such occasions', before leaving for Llawhaden, where he was on 10 September, Lamphey (12 September) and England.

Although no evidence survives as to the nature of the 'festival', we may surmise that the great hall was packed with canons and clergy, together with the bishop's officials and household. The courtyard would be full of their retainers and their horses.

No doubt all the fireplaces in the kitchen were kept fully employed for the feasting, with the servants passing along the corridors, bringing the choice dishes for the footsore bishop and his guests as they sat at the high table on the dais. We may imagine the best silver or even gold dishes and goblets gleaming on the tables; the brazier burning in the centre of the hall, its smoke escaping through the louvre on the roof; the September sun or the early moonlight beaming through the tall side windows and the great wheel window in the east gable.

HISTORY: THE LATER MIDDLE AGES

The scale of the feasting may be imagined from the evidence for an entertainment in the bishop's palace at Wells in 1337. On that occasion 268 people sat down to a feast of fish consisting of twenty congers, twenty cod and ling, eighteen pollack, thirty fresh and salted hake, four haddock, twenty-three sticks of eels, bream, gurnard, plaice, salmon, stockfish, a pike and a pickerel. All this was washed down with 86 gallons (391 litres) of second-class ale.

At St Davids in 1398, the bishop's slaughterhouse just outside the palace on the bank of the Alun, the dovecote in the angle of the close wall, and the brewhouse, were doubtless kept busy to provide such an entertainment for Bishop Guy and his guests.

Given the magnificence of the palace, it may be surprising to note that the medieval bishops of St Davids, by and large, seem to have spent their time elsewhere. When they were in the diocese they appear to have spent more time in their country seat at Lamphey (where the buildings were extended by Henry de Gower), or at the castle of Llawhaden, where the major administration of the diocese appears to have been carried out. Many episcopal wills are dated from these places. Outside the diocese they spent their time either at the episcopal lodging near St Bride's church (Bridewell) in London, convenient for Parliament, or at manor houses owned by them personally. Many of them also held ordinations elsewhere than at the cathedral.

As far as can be ascertained from the episcopal registers, the bishops came to St Davids for the great feasts of the church, such as Easter when they stayed over at the palace for the chapter meeting on Easter Monday. By the end of the fifteenth century their

The scale of the feasting at the bishop's palace can be imagined from contemporary descriptions of similar occasions. This late fifteenth-century manuscript illustration shows bishops and noblemen preparing to dine (© The British Library Board, Royal Ms. 14 E IV, f. 244v).

HISTORY: REFORMATION AND DECLINE

Right: By the middle of the fourteenth century, the bishops appear to have preferred to stay at Lamphey during their visits to the diocese, despite the magnificent arrangement of buildings achieved in the episcopal palace at St Davids (Skyscan Balloon Photography for Cadw).

Below: The seal of Richard Rawlins (1523–36), the last pre-Reformation bishop of St Davids. The figure to the left is probably St David, with his primatial cross. To the right is the figure of an abbess, perhaps a representation of St Non, the mother of St David (The National Archives: PRO, E 25/84, pt 1).

visits appear to have become increasingly infrequent, but this does not mean that the palace was wholly abandoned. In August 1493 Bishop Hugh Pavy (1485–95) appointed William Barstable to the office of 'keeper of our palace within the close of our cathedral church of St Davids' at the princely stipend of 8*d.* per annum. A few months later he was made apparitor-general of the diocese, which no doubt brought him a larger stipend. We may, therefore, conclude that the palace was kept on a care and maintenance basis for the greater part of the year by a skeleton staff.

Reformation and Decline

The 1530s saw a change in the fortunes of both the cathedral and the palace. Indeed, long before the Reformation, there are clear signs of growing impoverishment within the see. Economic difficulties in the fourteenth and fifteenth centuries meant that the bishops, apart from anything else, could no longer afford the upkeep of these large buildings in a relatively remote corner of the diocese. The financial situation was to become even worse in the sixteenth century.

HISTORY: REFORMATION AND DECLINE

In 1536, William Barlow became the first Protestant bishop of St Davids (1536–48). The changes brought about by the Reformation itself meant that, during Barlow's time, the cathedral lost its esteem as a centre of pilgrimage. For Barlow, too, St Davids became unsuited as a centre of Protestant preaching and also for the administration of the diocese.

Thus, as part of his programme for the theological reformation and better administration of the diocese, William Barlow urged Thomas Cromwell (d. 1540) to remove the see to Carmarthen. He failed in his intentions but, nevertheless, gained an unenviable reputation at St Davids. A commentator at the end of the sixteenth century laid the blame for the unroofing of the palace, 'for Lucre of the Lead', squarely at Barlow's door. Later tradition further maligned him in that it claimed that he did so in order to provide dowries for his five daughters. In fact, none of them had been born by this time.

It was, however, during Barlow's episcopate that the bishops of St Davids seem to have moved their chief residence to Abergwili outside Carmarthen, where they still reside. The probable reason for this was not so much the unroofing of the palace at St Davids but the loss of the manor of Lamphey, which Barlow was forced to surrender to the Crown in 1546. At the beginning of his episcopate, Barlow certainly spent some time at St Davids since in 1537 he had summoned the precentor of the cathedral to appear before him at the palace.

The evidence for what precise damage Barlow did to the structure is confusing. Sixteenth-century sources, quoted by later antiquaries, seem to suggest that he removed the roofs from the whole of the palace, though some may have been replaced. Bishop Milbourne's licence for demolition makes it plain that by 1616 the state apartments had been unroofed for at least a century, which raises the intriguing possibility that a bishop earlier than Barlow had been responsible for the dismantling. On balance, however, it does seem likely that Barlow removed the roof over the south range, that covering the great hall and chamber (pp. 37–40).

There is evidence from the episcopal registers and chapter records that bishops continued to use parts of the palace when they came to St Davids for ordinations and visitations. Bishop Robert Ferrar (1548–54) states that he came 'home' to St Davids where he commenced his visitation; Bishop Henry Morgan (1554–59) was certainly in residence in 1556; and Richard Davies (1561–81) conducted an ordination there in 1564. Moreover, Marmaduke Middleton (1582–94) appears to have resided there regularly, and complained of its cold situation.

In the seventeenth century, the trend towards decay presumably continued. It is worth noting, however, that the earliest representation of the palace — seen in John Speed's map of Pembrokeshire (1610) — shows that part of the structure was apparently still roofed. The wing opening out from the rear of the great chamber, the wing to the east of the bishop's chamber and the area between the two halls thus appear to have been habitable, together with the episcopal apartments. This said, in his description of the palace, Speed stated that although it was a 'goodly house ... all of free stone', [its] 'uncovered tops cause the curious workes in the walles daily to weepe and them [the canons] to fear their downfalle ere long'.

In 1616 Bishop Milbourne (1615–21) applied to Archbishop Abbott for a licence to demolish both the castle of Llawhaden and certain buildings within the palace at St Davids. The commission appointed by the archbishop of Canterbury to investigate the

The seal of William Barlow (1536–48), first Protestant bishop of St Davids. Barlow failed to persuade Thomas Cromwell to remove the see from its ancient location to Carmarthen (The National Archives: PRO, C 107/186 pt 2).

Below: John Speed's plan of St Davids in 1610. It shows that parts of the palace buildings, to the left of the cathedral, were still roofed with lead as well as slate (National Library of Wales).

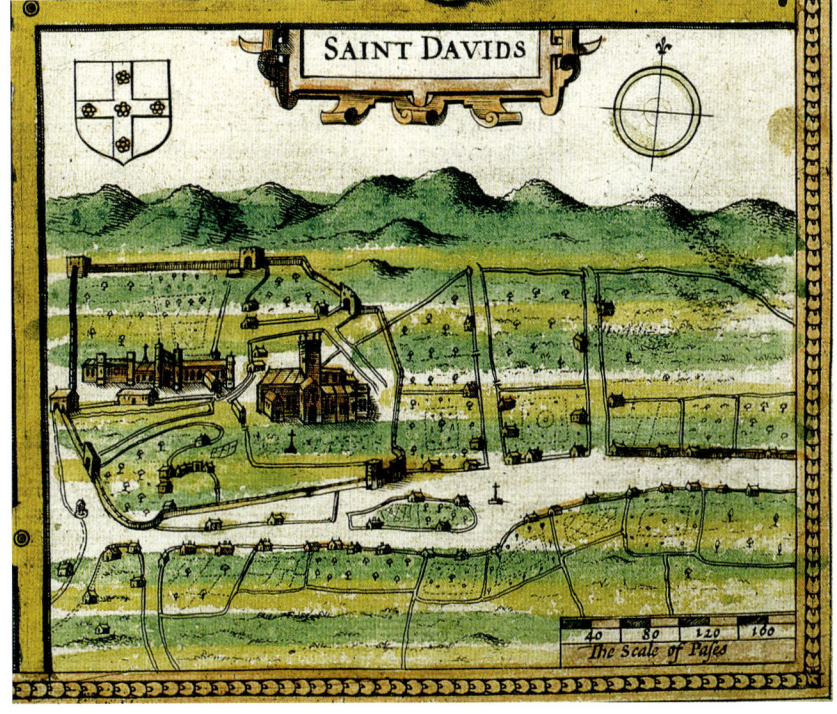

HISTORY: REFORMATION AND DECLINE

Right: Bishop William Laud (1621–27), who appears to have considered repairing parts of the palace. He is known to have visited the diocese twice, staying at St Davids in 1622, but choosing Brecon and Abergwili on his second visit in 1625. Laud later became archbishop of Canterbury (1633–45); he was executed in 1645, during the Civil War (National Portrait Gallery, London).

Far right: Bishop William Thomas (1677–83), who sought further licence from the archbishop of Canterbury to demolish the palace. Although the licence was granted, it is clear from what remains today that total demolition did not take place (Carmarthen Museum).

state of the building reported in May 1616 that there were in 'the manor or mansion commonly called the palace of St Davids a certain ruined hall commonly called the royal brewhouse and a bakehouse', which had been in ruins for a hundred years. Accordingly, the archbishop issued a licence in June 1616 for the demolition of all these structures. From the state of the surviving apartments, however, no major demolition seems to have been carried out.

Milbourne's successor was William Laud (1621–27), later archbishop of Canterbury until his execution in 1645. In 1621 a survey of the palace was undertaken for the bishop with a view to repairing it. Although it is difficult to ascertain precisely which parts of the palace were being considered, it would seem that the west wing and the episcopal apartments were maintained in repair.

Laud himself came to St Davids, and presumably stayed at the palace on 24 and 25 July 1622. On his second visit to this diocese in 1625, he does not appear to have come to St Davids but stayed instead at Brecon and Abergwili. The last positive evidence for the use of the palace by a bishop appears to be on 27 July 1633 when Laud's successor, Theophilus Field (1627–35), held a chapter meeting there.

During the Commonwealth, all the episcopal lands and manors were sequestrated. A document bearing on the sale of the lands around St Davids in 1651 refers to the palace as a 'capital messuage', which would seem to imply that it was still habitable. Some time later, probably in 1659 or 1660, a schedule of the episcopal lands was drawn up in which the palace is referred to as 'part in repayre'. Nevertheless, when the first Restoration bishop of St Davids, William Lucy (1660–77), commissioned a survey of all the episcopal possessions in 1660, the palace is not mentioned at all.

In 1670–71, Bishop Lucy brought a suit against one Henry Williams, in which it was stated that the bishop had demised to Williams 'all that decayed pallace of St Davids' and its appurtenances on 19 July 1661, in as large a manner as James Matthias Esq. had held the same. The reason for this suit, however, was an attempt by the bishop to recover damages from the tenant because he had allowed 'one hall, one parlour, and two chambers' to become uncovered — unroofed. This sounds as if Williams had given the *coup de grâce* to the episcopal apartments on the east side of the courtyard, and this appears to mark the final chapter in the story of the palace as an active residence.

During the episcopate of William Thomas (1677–83), presumably as part of his intention of moving the see to Carmarthen, another licence to demolish the palace was sought from the archbishop of Canterbury. The licence was issued on 6 April 1678

HISTORY: REFORMATION AND DECLINE

but, again, given the substantial nature of the present ruins, it is clear that total demolition was not carried out. By the time Adam Ottley became bishop (1713–23), and an episcopal residence at St Davids was mooted, it was the treasury and not the palace which was contemplated as his dwelling. In the event, Ottley spent large sums on the refurbishment of the palace at Abergwili, which appears to have become the main residence of the bishops of St Davids.

For the remainder of the eighteenth century, the palace was described as 'decayed', though several poor families are known to have lodged in cottages built within the ruins. From the end of that century, and on into the 1800s, the palace and its grounds were let as a market garden. A print of 1810 shows the interior of the great hall being cultivated for this purpose.

Some small attempt was made at restoration, or rather consolidation, of the palace by Sir George Gilbert Scott (1811–78) — or perhaps one of his sons — during a major restoration of the cathedral in the latter part of the nineteenth century. Evidence of this can be seen in parts of the arcaded parapet and in the gatehouse. In 1929, the dean and chapter issued an appeal for £20,000 for the cathedral and its ruined buildings. In the event, consolidation and preservation were carried out not by the dean and his chapter but by HM Commissioners for Works, under whose guardianship the ruins were placed by the Representative Body of the Church in Wales in 1932. In the 1940s, the close wall was conveyed to the Ministry of Public Building and Works, and today both palace and wall are maintained by Cadw, the historic environment service of the Welsh Government.

From early in the eighteenth century the bishop's palace was described as 'decayed', though it became popular with a number of artists who visited St Davids and painted the neglected buildings. This 1775 print by Paul Sandby (1730/31–1809) is in the 'Picturesque' tradition, and shows the already ruinous buildings from the south-east (National Library of Wales).

A Tour of the Palace

The Plan and Construction of the Palace

Before beginning your tour of the various apartments, stand (or perhaps sit down) in the courtyard in order to appreciate the overall plan of the palace. With your back to the ticket office, you can examine the principal ranges of buildings around the quadrangle, each one representing a main phase of construction.

To your right, the west range is the earliest building surviving on the site, and probably dates from the early thirteenth century. Long and narrow, with tall gable ends, it must be the *mansio* fit only 'for servants and animals' described in the survey of 1327 (p. 14). It was later to be modified by Bishop Henry de Gower to provide lodgings.

The northern side of the courtyard — that which is behind you — is closed off with the precinct wall, and includes a three-storey gatehouse retaining traces of its battlements. The wall itself extended around the whole of the palace, including its gardens and orchards, and also joined up with the main wall surrounding the cathedral close as a whole (pp. 48–49). The palace wall and gatehouse may have been built following Bishop Bek's instruction of 1287 in which he ordered the canons to enclose their houses.

On your left, the east range contains the bishop's hall, together with his solar or private chamber, which has a further wing running out at right angles to the rear. These were the first buildings to be completed during the episcopate of Bishop Henry de Gower, from 1328 to 1347, and were always intended to serve as his private apartments. The work represents the first phase in Gower's step-by-step creation of an entirely new residence.

Directly ahead lies the south range, where, beyond an extraordinarily elaborate porch, there is a great hall, marked by its three tall window openings.

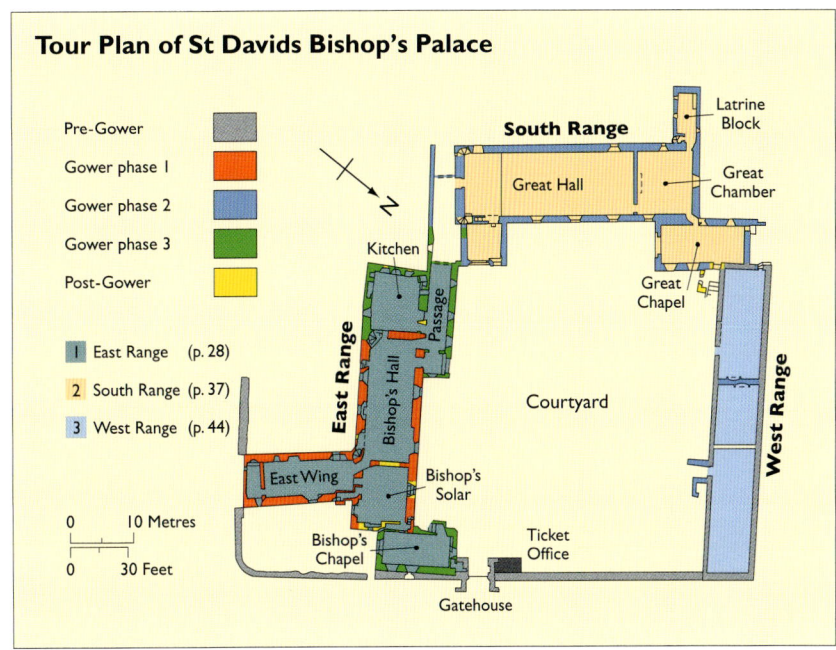

A great chapel, contemporary with the hall, stands in the right-hand corner, between the south and the west ranges. In all, the south range marks the second phase of Henry de Gower's overall plan. It housed the grander ceremonial apartments in which church feasts might be held, and was also where the more important guests and distinguished pilgrims to St Davids might be welcomed and accommodated.

The final phase in the creation of Gower's palace involved the construction of a first-floor passage, linking the east and south ranges. The work included a new porch added to the front of the bishop's hall, with a distinctive semi-octagonal-headed doorway. A remarkable new kitchen was also built behind the passage; and the bishop's private chapel, tucked in rather awkwardly between the east range and the gatehouse, is probably of much the same date. This phase is also marked by the arcaded parapet, which was added to the already existing bishop's hall and solar.

Opposite: Henry de Gower transformed the bishop's palace with the construction of two separate ranges of accommodation, distinguished today by their distinctive arcaded parapets. That to the east (foreground) was for the bishop's private use and that to the south (left) was used to receive distinguished guests and pilgrims. The now ruined west range, which was probably first built in the thirteenth century, was also modified by Bishop Henry to provide storage and more modest lodgings.

The East Range

The Porch to the Bishop's Hall

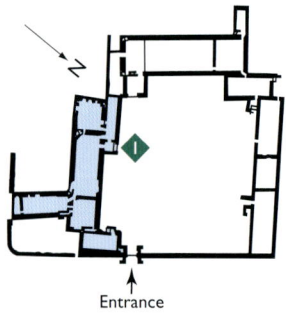

Only minor changes and additions were subsequently made to Gower's grand design. Standing in the courtyard, only two of these can be readily seen. To the far right, in the angle between the great chapel and the west range, a small porch was added; and to the left, part of the window in the bishop's solar was blocked.

As completed, Gower's palace operated at two levels. The first floor was where the bishop and his guests lived, ate, prayed, were entertained and slept. At ground-floor level, a series of undercrofts provided storage for food, beer, wine, and fuel. The undercrofts also provided some accommodation and work rooms for the servants. The two levels were connected by six intermural staircases by which servants would have moved up and down carrying meals, drinks, empty dishes, and logs for the fires. There were three more staircases rising from first-floor level, eventually reaching a point high above all the other buildings of the cathedral close, on the wall-walks above the handsome arcaded parapet.

The tour suggests one route around the bishop's palace, beginning with the rooms at first-floor level and concluding with the undercrofts and the exterior of the main ranges. But it is not intended to be rigid and visitors may investigate the various parts of the palace in any order using the bird's-eye view (inside front cover) or the ground plan (inside back cover) as a guide.

The doorway (which did not contain a door) has a very distinctive semi-octagonal head. Although only four of the stones in the arch are medieval, these were sufficient to allow for an accurate reconstruction of the original form, with the work completed in 1993. The style of the doorway itself is rather unusual, though there is another example in the cathedral pulpitum screen. It is interesting that the form also occurs in the porch of the great hall at Berkeley Castle in Gloucestershire. The Berkeley doorway was probably completed about 1343–45, and the two examples might well be the work of the same master mason.

Here, on the left-hand side, note the short section of an outer order of stones decorated with flower ornament [A]. Once through the doorway, looking up you will see the scars of a quadripartite stone vault which would have formed the porch ceiling. The door directly ahead leads into the bishop's hall. From there, continue to the kitchen.

Opposite: Steps lead up to the carefully restored doorway of the porch to the bishop's hall. The similarities with the doorway in the porch to the great hall at Berkeley Castle, Gloucestershire (below right), which was probably completed about 1343–45, suggest they may be the work of the same master mason (David Price/BCCT).

Below: The palace courtyard, with the ruinous west range in the foreground and the south and east ranges beyond. The west range probably represents the earliest work at the site, though it was later remodelled by Bishop Henry de Gower.

TOUR: THE EAST RANGE

Right: At first-floor level, the kitchen was divided into roughly equal quarters by low segmental arches carried on a central octagonal pier. The springer stones for these arches are still visible in the kitchen walls and the position of the pier is marked by a timber replica.

Below: The palace kitchen was once a remarkable room; this reconstruction drawing shows how it may have looked in the middle of the fourteenth century (Illustration by Chris Jones-Jenkins, 1999).

The Kitchen

This kitchen belongs to the last phase of Bishop Henry de Gower's work. It replaces an earlier example which was situated on the ground floor, wrapped around the southern end of the bishop's hall. The master mason set himself a real challenge in building the new kitchen, for the plan of the room is not quite square and it was to incorporate parts of the earlier structure.

As completed, the ground floor was filled with three stone vaults. Above these, at the level of the modern timber floor, the room was divided into four roughly equal quarters, separated one from another by low segmental arches. The springer stones for these arches survive in the side walls, and they were carried centrally on an octagonal stone pier, now marked by a timber replica.

Subconical vaults were constructed in each quadrant, and were drawn together into two pairs of chimneys on the ridge of the roof. The vaults acted as hoods to draw away the heat, smoke and cooking smells from the open fires or charcoal braziers set out on the original stone floor. It was here that the huge quantities of food for the episcopal feasts were cooked (pp. 20–21).

The windows are set high in the walls to let light down on to the working areas. In the east wall there is a mural recess, perhaps some form of oven, and the drain through which the kitchen slops could be poured away. The south wall has an ordinary fireplace and a domed cupboard. There is another domed cupboard in the west wall to the left of the door. To the right of the door are the remains of a hatch through which finished dishes were passed to servants waiting to take the food along the passage towards whichever of the two halls was in use.

Follow the route of one of these servants back along the passage and into the bishop's hall.

The Bishop's Hall 3

Just inside, you should imagine a fourteenth-century wooden screen hiding this southern end from the main part of the hall. The position of the screen is marked by a line of slate in the floor. The servants would have come in from the passageway and perhaps paused behind the screen before progressing into the hall proper. The screen would also have hidden two doorways. One led to a spiral staircase down to the undercroft, and another led to stairs up to the parapet walkway. The passage created by the screen was probably covered with a ceiling, set into the deep sockets in the wall behind.

Should you care to, from this point there is an opportunity to climb up to the parapet. Half-way up there is an alcove within the thickness of the wall, which looks back into the hall. Perhaps one of the palace staff may have sat here in relative secret, watching or listening to what was going on in the hall.

The bishop's hall looking towards the screen end of the chamber. Servants approaching from the passageway would perhaps have paused behind the screen before entering the hall proper. The small window, high up in the end wall, gave an excellent view of the proceedings below.

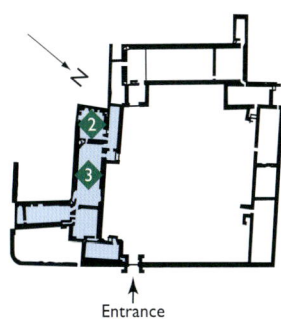

Right: Two of the windows that lit the bishop's hall on the east side. The windows were glazed at the top and closed with shutters at the bottom.

Far right: Two of the finely carved corbels, each depicting a human head, which once supported the wooden roof trusses in the bishop's hall (top) and in the bishop's solar (below).

The now ruinous fireplace on the courtyard side of the bishop's hall originally rose to a tall chequerboard-decorated chimney, as shown in this illustration, which appeared in the study of St Davids by W. B. Jones and E. A. Freeman (1856).

Alternatively, the alcove may have functioned rather like a pulpit, with one of the cathedral clerics reading to the assembled company.

At the top of the staircase, you will see just how narrow the walkway was. There is also a corner turret with its own staircase to the roof, providing an even more elevated standpoint. Back in the hall proper, notice a small doorway directly opposite the entrance from the porch. This would have led down into a lean-to structure against the outer side of the range.

The main part of the bishop's hall was well lit by a series of tall windows fitted with stone seats in the reveals. The upper halves of the windows were glazed, whereas the lower parts might be closed off with wooden shutters. The bishop would have sat behind a table at the far, or dais, end of the hall. This area was covered with a wooden canopy carried on a line of five carved corbels set into the end wall. Only the corbel in the left-hand corner survives. To either side of the dais position, there was a single-light window, with the remains of the tracery surviving in the blocked example which looked towards the cathedral. To the right of the dais, another spiral stair gave access to a different section of the undercrofts. The hall fireplace is near the dais on the courtyard side. Originally, the fireplace flue rose to a tall circular chimney, known from illustrations to have been decorated with a chequerboard pattern. The chimney fell in about 1850 (though it appears in an engraving published in 1856). The walls within the hall were certainly plastered, though there is no evidence for painted decoration. Overhead, the great wooden roof trusses were carried on stone corbels set into the side walls and featuring carved heads. The serenity of the figures contrasts markedly with the sculpture incorporated in the parapet outside (pp. 42–43).

When you have finished here, pass through the door at the dais end of the hall and turn right into the east wing.

East Wing

One of the bishop's two private chambers was located on the upper floor of the east wing. It probably served as his bedchamber, usually described in the Middle Ages as a parlour. The east wing itself is lower than the main part of the range; its upper walls did not carry the full arcaded parapet seen elsewhere. Instead, there is a plain, blind arcade, with castellations above, best viewed from the exterior.

On entering, to the immediate right you will see the base of a staircase which gave access to the level above the dais canopy in the bishop's hall. The base of the staircase is lit by an unusual window. Though largely restored in the nineteenth century, you can see how the wooden shutter would have slid horizontally into the wall.

The fireplace, with its tall circular chimney, is situated opposite the main window midway along the southern wall. The far end of the room was screened off from the remainder and housed a latrine. What appears as a second tall circular chimney is in fact a vent for the latrine pit below. In the opposite corner, there is a blocked doorway which led to the walkway on the precinct wall.

Turning about, from this vantage point there are good views of the details in the arcaded parapet. From here, you should progress directly into the bishop's solar through the right-hand door.

The Bishop's Solar 5

The solar was the bishop's private sitting room, where only his closest friends would have been entertained. You will see signs that it was a once handsome chamber. Almost square in plan, it has a massive fireplace in the northern gable wall, and was lit by two windows of the same design as those in the adjacent hall. Note the fine colonnettes and delicate capitals which adorn the inner jambs (rear-arches) of the window splays and more decorative corbels depicting human heads. The doorway to the right of the window in the east wall led to a private latrine set in the passage in the wall.

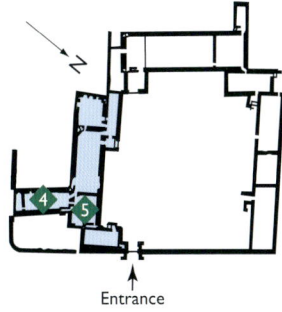

A view from the east wing towards the bishop's hall and solar. The room in the east wing — which contains a massive fireplace — may have served as the bishop's bedchamber.

The solar was the one room in the palace which was substantially altered during the later Middle Ages. A new floor was inserted, with the beams set in sockets cut just below the wall tops. Part of the window overlooking the courtyard was blocked, and a doorway was created at high level in the northern gable end. Access into this new upper storey was from the same staircase in the east wing which led up to the dais canopy. The bishops of St Davids were last documented using the palace in the seventeenth century. By this time, although many chambers had been abandoned, the converted solar was probably still in use.

Next is the bishop's chapel which is approached through the small servants' doorway in the north-west corner and then a narrow modern breach in the wall beyond.

The Bishop's Chapel

This room has generally been identified as a chapel. It is orientated east to west and had windows that were fully glazed. There was no fireplace, and there must have been an elegant wooden ceiling carried on the alternating large and small carved-head corbels. The altar would have been located beneath the large east window. However, it is rather plainer than the great chapel in the opposite corner of the courtyard (pp. 40–41). You should note, too, that the original entrance was by way of an external flight of steps, not through the breach in the wall you have just used.

Turning to look up at the gable end of the solar, you will see that the chapel was an addition, probably built during the third phase of Gower's work. The doorway situated at high level was inserted later still and gave access from the solar into an upper gallery or pew, with a view down into the chapel.

Before the door was inserted, the chapel was probably for the use of the bishop's servants and his immediate retinue. Only after the conversion of the solar did the bishop himself have private access into the building.

You should next approach the great hall located across the courtyard in the south range, where the bishop's distinguished guests would have entered via the magnificent porch.

Above: The bishop's solar was once a handsome chamber, equipped with a large fireplace in its north gable wall. The small doorway alongside it allowed servants to wait on the bishop and his close friends assembled here in private.

Right: This mid-fifteenth-century manuscript illustration of an author at work in his study gives some sense of the comfortable surroundings that the bishop's private chambers may have provided (© Bibliothèque royale de Belgique, Brussels, Ms. 9278–80, f. 10r).

The bishop's chapel, set between the gatehouse and the bishop's solar, was approached by steps from the courtyard and entered through the large arched opening that housed both a doorway and a window.

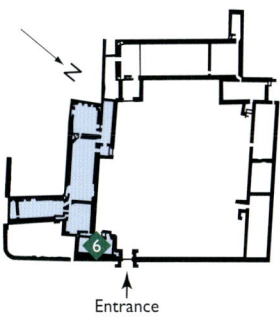

Entrance

Recent Conservation at the Bishop's Palace

In 2010, Cadw's team of highly skilled craftspeople completed a fifteen-year programme of conservation at the palace to rectify centuries of decay and to restore key decorative features.

In the fourteenth century, Bishop Gower's masons used a range of local stones for the rubble walls and the carved decorative stonework. To unify the design the walls were rendered and painted. Where the render has worn away, some of the softer stones have been very badly eroded. In some areas, it has been necessary to replace the medieval masonry to ensure structural stability; in other areas, render has been re-applied.

The local purple Caerbwdi sandstone was selected by the medieval masons for sculpture and for dressed stonework — around doors and windows, for example. It weathers badly and cracks easily. By studying the moulded and carved details cut in this stone, it is possible to identify the 'signatures' of the different masons who built the palace and link them to regional 'schools' where they learnt their trade. To ensure the structural stability of some of the openings and the survival of the masons' 'signatures', a number of stones have been newly carved and replaced in the walls.

The sculptured stonework is very precious and cannot be accurately restored. Pins and glues have been used to hold the laminating stonework together and coloured lime mortars used to fill in pockets caused by erosion. Parts of the chequerboard parapet have been restored by piecing in squares of purple and yellow stone. The quality of this conservation work was recognized when the project received a European Union Prize for Cultural Heritage from Europa Nostra — the pan-European federation of cultural heritage — in 2010.

Conservation work is essential to preserve the palace. Recent work includes the replacement of badly eroded dressed stonework with new stones carved to the original profile. Examples of renewed stonework may be found in the great hall porch (below left) and the bishop's solar (below).

The South Range

The Great Hall Porch 7

The bishop's palace at St Davids was raised in the Decorated style of medieval Gothic architecture, and it is the porch leading into the great hall which was undoubtedly the most highly decorated part of the building. As the first part of the palace to be seen when entering the courtyard, we can be sure that the features of the porch were designed to impress.

The rubble walls of both the porch and the great hall itself were completely rendered, and there is evidence that this render coating was painted red. Above what must have been an already striking façade, the walls were crowned with the most elaborate form of the arcaded parapet, with figure corbels at two levels and carved tablet flowers on the arches. Higher still, the spandrels over the arches and the now lost parapet were adorned with a chequerboard pattern in yellow and purple stone.

The arch above the doorway is of a wide depressed ogee (S-shaped) form, with lines of very eroded leaves and carved vine ornament running around the complex moulding profile. Seaweed foliage covers the two capitals, and also the central finial. Above the arch, there are two gabled and crocketted statue niches. You will see stone ribs carved in the heads of the niches. All that remains of the statues are the lower parts of two seated and draped figures. Traditionally, these have been identified as King Edward III (1327–77) and Queen Philippa (d. 1369), though this is by no means certain.

The Great Hall 8

The great hall was clearly a very large and imposing room, certainly by medieval standards. Measuring some 88 feet (27m) long by 29 feet (9m) wide, the entire internal space was open to the closely set wooden trusses of the roof, with the apex of these trusses rising to about 40 feet (12.5m) high.

Close to the entrance from the porch, a staircase within the thickness of the wall led up to the wall-walk. Nearby, in what are the two eastern corners of the room (left as you enter), doorways give access to further staircases leading down to the undercrofts below. At this same end of the range, a central

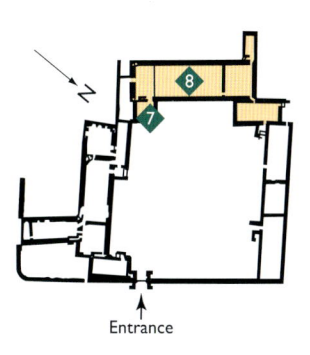

A drawing of the finely carved leaves and vine ornament — now very eroded — on the doorway of the great hall porch from the 1856 study of St Davids by W. B. Jones and E. A. Freeman.

Left: The great hall looking east towards the wheel window.

Opposite: The great hall porch is the most highly decorated part of the palace and would no doubt have impressed visitors on their arrival in the courtyard. The remains of two statues can still be seen in the niches above the doorway; they are traditionally thought to represent King Edward III (1327–77) and Queen Philippa (d. 1369), though this is by no means certain.

One of the two crude sockets in the side walls of the great hall, which indicate the position of a possible second screen.

Below: A reconstruction of how the great hall may have looked in about 1350. The wooden screen was positioned so that it hid servants approaching from the kitchen, or from the undercrofts below the great hall. The bishop and his guests would have sat at the high table at the opposite, or dais, end of the hall (Illustration by Terry Ball, 1991; with modifications, 1999).

doorway connects with the passage to and from the kitchen. All in all, we must imagine a scene where food is brought in by servants arriving in procession from the kitchen, with wine and other drink arriving from the undercrofts by one staircase, and with the used dishes and waste taken back down via the other. But it is important to remember that these three doorways would have been hidden from the hall proper by a decorative wooden screen, the location of which is marked by slates set into the floor and by the two scribed lines to be seen in the plaster a little below the raised window in the south wall. There may have been a second wooden screen just beyond the step in the hall floor. In this case, the crude sockets cut into the base of each side wall probably indicate its position.

As you approach the dais or high table end of the hall — marked by the low cross-wall — note three windows overlooking the courtyard. These are of a very similar design to those in the bishop's hall. They were glazed above and shuttered below, with stone seats in the reveals. Here, however, the rear-arches do not have the delicate colonnettes seen in the east range, but instead they feature a simple continuous wave moulding. To your left, the opposite wall is blank apart from the single window which lit the high table itself.

All of the rubble stone in the walls was covered in plaster, and, although there are no signs of elaborate painted decoration, a fragment of a yellow ochre wash has been identified in the adjacent great chamber. Moreover, the long blank southern wall, as well as the now-lost partition wall behind the dais, would have allowed for rich woven or tapestry hangings, adding colour and warmth to the entire room. There were no fireplaces in the walls so the hall must have been heated by a central hearth, marked by modern pitched stone, with a louvred chimney in the roof above to allow the smoke to escape. Somewhat old-fashioned by the fourteenth century, such an arrangement may have increased the drama and the sense of feasting in an ancient hall.

When you reach the dais end of the hall, turn around and look back at the very attractive wheel window set below the gable in the east wall. Carved in limestone quarried in the Bath region, the composition is made up of sixteen radiating 'daggers' set around a central quatrefoil. In turn, the wheel is set within two moulded rings of purple Caerbwdi sandstone. Notice that the outer ring — carved with flat or tablet flowers — has a pronounced eccentric curve. It would appear that Bishop Henry de Gower's master mason deliberately adopted this form so as to create an optical illusion: he knew that when it was viewed from below it would look perfectly circular. The window itself was doubtless filled with painted glass, and we can perhaps imagine the morning sun casting a great pool of colour on the tiled floor of the great hall.

During a great feast, the bishop's chair would have been positioned on the dais platform, immediately in front of the now ruined cross-wall. Only his most distinguished guests and household staff would have sat alongside him at the high table. Above them hung a rich fabric canopy, and the table would have been covered with a white linen tablecloth. All the best dishes of silver and gold, together with cups and flagons, were laid out on a buffet to one side. The remaining guests, and members of the bishop's retinue, would have sat on benches at tables ranged down the length of the room. The servants who carried the food from the kitchen were met at the far wooden screen by the steward. Holding his rod of office, he led them in procession up to the high table. Here, further servants in special household uniform or livery — the carver, the cupbearer and the sewer (or server) — were waiting to serve the meal. Several courses known as messes were served, all in a prescribed fashion. The bishop was the first to be attended to, followed by the remainder of the high table, and then the other guests sat along the length of the hall. Food was prepared in such quantities (p. 21), enough would generally be left over for the servants; it might also go to the poor gathered at the precinct gates.

From this end of the hall, pass through the doorway in the ruined cross-wall into the great chamber.

Above: One window lit the dais in the great hall. It would have been glazed at the top and closed at the bottom with wooden shutters. Part of the mullion has been replaced.

Above left: The Bath-stone wheel window in the great hall, set within a moulded frame of purple Caerbwdi stone.

Left: This early fourteenth-century manuscript illustration shows a procession of servants bearing dishes to the high table. No doubt similar scenes would have been familiar in the great hall of the bishop's palace (© The British Library Board, Royal Ms. 2 B VII, f. 200r).

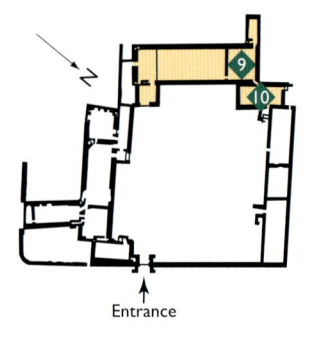

The Great Chamber

In terms of layout, the great chamber occupies much the same position as the bishop's solar in the east range. Occasionally, it would have served as a private sitting room and bedchamber for an important guest to St Davids. At other times it may have been used by the bishop and important members of his clergy, perhaps as a retreat away from those more public ceremonies still in progress in the great hall. But we should remember that both secular and ecclesiastical lords would not retreat to such a private chamber to eat on a regular basis. Indeed, unless he was sick or especially weary, the bishop of St Davids would generally have been anxious to show himself in his hall at meal times, reinforcing his position as the head of the palace household.

The great chamber was lit by windows in each of the outer walls, and heated by a fireplace against the cross-wall. The doorway in the south-west corner leads into a small extension, now restored with a lavatory seat and urinal at the far end set over a cesspit that could be cleaned out at ground level. A narrow staircase leads to a small bedchamber above the latrine and to an alcove overlooking the great chamber, just as in the bishop's hall.

There are small turrets at three corners of this range with two more on the outer side of the east range. All of them have narrow staircases which gave access out on to their roofs. These turrets may have served as vantage points, where servants in livery might have added to the drama of the occasion when the bishop or important guests arrived at the cathedral precinct. Trumpets may have been used, for example, to herald a welcome.

From the base of the stairs, cross the great chamber to the opposite corner. You will find a short, narrow passage leading into the great chapel.

The Great Chapel

The roof of the passage which leads from the great chamber is made up of slabs of stone that are corbelled in circular fashion to form a domed vault, a technique that can be seen elsewhere in the palace. Notice, too, that the door into the chapel was closed and locked from the passage side.

Originally, there was no other entrance, which means the chapel was only accessible to those important enough to have entered the great hall and the great chamber. In contrast, as noted above (p. 34), access to the bishop's chapel was by way of a staircase directly from the courtyard.

Here in the great chapel, the altar stood below what was a three-light east window. The exterior jambs of this window are flanked by statue niches. Inside, to the right of the window, there is a purple sandstone piscina, a significant liturgical fitting used by the celebrant to wash the communion vessels at Mass. The hole in the sill leads to a drain beneath. Now restored, the piscina is a jewel of the Decorated style of ornament, with graceful crockets and vine leaf carving crowning a complex moulded frame. Indeed, the details of the design compare well with those in Bishop Henry de

The latrine housed in the small extension off the great chamber.

Right: The elaborately carved piscina in the great chapel. The details are similar to Henry de Gower's work in the cathedral.

Gower's work in the cathedral Lady Chapel, as well as on the pulpitum screen he had constructed at the east end of the nave. The now-bare stonework of the piscina would have been entirely covered with paint. There may well have been an illustration of a saint on the flat rear panel, as survives in a near contemporary piscina at Prior Crauden's chapel within the great cathedral-priory complex at Ely in Cambridgeshire.

All of the chapel windows were glazed, probably with stained glass. Moreover, further colour was given to the interior with multicolour figurative designs on the walls. Traces of paintwork survive in the heads of the two windows overlooking the courtyard.

Above the west gable of the chapel, the north-west corner is crowned with a small belfry which in turn carries a broached spirelet. Two bells were hung in the belfry, and were rung by way of ropes hanging down into the chapel through the two square sockets.

Before you leave the chapel, you may care to stand on the wooden steps below the east window and look at the line of corbels on the great hall parapet. They are described on the interpretation panel (also see p. 42).

The doorway inserted in the courtyard wall of the chapel was a late medieval modification. In fact, there is other evidence to suggest that the great chapel remained in use for some time after the unroofing of the remainder of the south range.

The great chapel seen across the courtyard from the bishop's hall.

A section of the arcaded parapet on the great chapel, supported by corbels carved in the shape of recognizable, if exotic, creatures. These figures face into the courtyard and contrast both with the monstrous creatures that feature on the exterior corbels of the east range and with the serene human faces that adorn the interior of the bishop's apartments. It has been suggested that these differences reflect the contrast between outer darkness or chaos, and inner light or order — concepts that are typical of the opposites which governed medieval thought.

Sculpted Decoration and the Arcaded Parapet

Above: Corbels in the shape of human heads are most often found inside the palace buildings. This woman's head is in the bishop's chapel.

Right: A corbel on the courtyard face of the great hall carved to represent a lion fighting a dog.

In all, Bishop Henry de Gower incorporated just under two hundred individual sculptures within the bishop's palace. There were six large statues — of which only the remains of the two seated figures in the niches on the great hall porch survive — but the majority comprised a remarkable collection of carved corbels. These can be divided into several groups, with human heads set into some of the interiors, and a mixture of human heads, animals and mythical creatures incorporated within the arcaded parapet.

Carved heads survive in the bishop's hall (where they supported the roof trusses and the dais canopy), the bishop's solar (where some were reset in later alterations), the bishop's chapel (where the ceiling was carried on alternating large and small heads), and there is a single example carrying the belfry in the great chapel. A variety of hair styles and head dresses can be seen, and some of the figures are bearded. At least four of the figures are women. The faces are of two generalized types, with no strong individual character, suggesting that they were not carved from life. By the 1330s, the use of human heads to support roof trusses was well established in the main rooms of great houses and so it is not surprising to see them adopted here.

Much more surprising is the mixed imagery depicted on the external corbels. It is similar to that found in illuminated manuscripts, in stained glass and on misericords. There are 149 corbels within the arcades of the parapet, though fifty-three of these are now eroded beyond recognition.

Apart from human heads, there are various animals. The commonest are lions, usually heads, but one is winged and there is a double-bodied corner corbel on the great chapel. There are two monkeys, a baboon (in the angle between the great hall and its porch) and an ape. There are three different types of dog, one cat, and an owl. Six of the corbels feature more than one creature, including a sow suckling piglets and a lion fighting a dog, both to be seen on the great hall.

The final group of at least fourteen corbels consists of hybrids, grotesques and mythical creatures. Five of these have human heads and crouching animal bodies, and another five are *grylli* — human hybrids with bat-like wings. There are three bird sirens and a mermaid or fish siren. Nearly all these monstrous creatures are found on the outside of the east range. The corbels in the parapet are most easily seen from the step provided in the great chapel (p. 41), and from within the east wing behind the solar (p. 33).

No other medieval domestic building has so much sculpture richly applied, though examples of the same images may be found in contemporary ecclesiastical buildings such as Exeter Cathedral and York Minster. In the fourteenth century, marvels and grotesques were as much part of religious teaching as saints and angels. Here at St Davids, the disposition of the sculpture may not be haphazard. As visitors approached the palace from the cathedral to the east, they were confronted with grotesques and monsters. On entering the courtyard, they saw recognizable if often exotic creatures, and on moving into the bishop's apartments they were overlooked by serene human faces. So they progressed from outer darkness to inner light, from chaos to order, typical of the opposites which governed medieval thought.

The arcaded parapet provided the opportunity for the display of this sculpture, and it was complemented by the chequerboard decoration or diaper work, a device used for wall decoration quite widely at this time. The parapet does have certain functional qualities, since it anchors the roof trusses and allows water to flow freely off the vast roofs, but its defensive appearance is purely for show. At times, trumpeters standing on top of the turrets in the bishop's livery may have appeared as 'living sculptures' (p. 40).

A mermaid-shaped corbel on the great chapel, overlooking the courtyard.

One of the corbels on the great chapel, sadly cut away to accommodate the roof line of the later medieval porch.

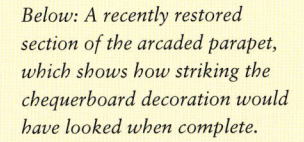

Below: A recently restored section of the arcaded parapet, which shows how striking the chequerboard decoration would have looked when complete.

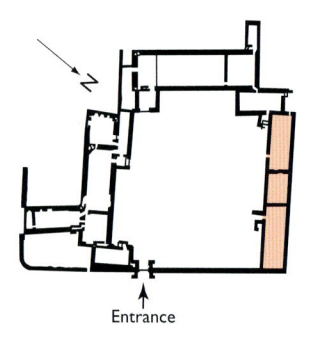

Two roof lines can be seen on the north wall of the great chapel. One marks the steeply pitched roof of the earlier west range and a second shows the line of the pent roof of the porch built against the chapel during the later Middle Ages.

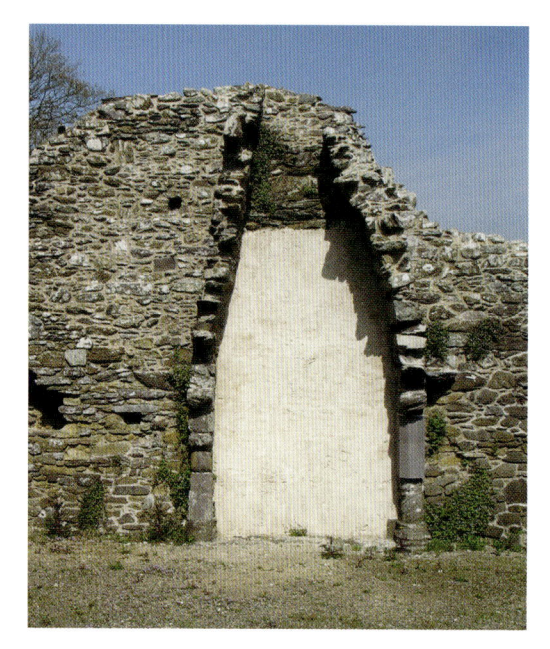

One of the two fireplaces against the cross-wall on the upper floor of the west range. Each fireplace was provided with a pair of stone lamp brackets.

The West Range

Outside the chapel doorway, a flight of steps leads back down to the courtyard. A porch was added here — between the great chapel and the west range — sometime during the later Middle Ages. Looking at the chapel wall, note how one of the corbels has been cut away to accommodate the roof line of the porch. Notice, too, the mermaid corbel, to the left.

Looking to the left from the top of the steps, you will have a good view along the full length of the west range. Probably first raised in the early thirteenth century, it was modified during Henry de Gower's fourteenth-century transformation of the palace. Stone vaults were inserted into the ground floor, and two long rooms created above. Fireplaces were set back to back in the partition wall between the two rooms. There are stone lamp brackets to either side of both fireplaces. From the nearer room, there was access into a latrine situated in the lean-to structure at the back of the great chapel.

Taken as a whole, the evidence suggests an early form of medieval lodgings. The accommodation was doubtless intended for guests of lower status, and the rooms were probably more like dormitories rather than the individual cellular lodgings which became common from the late fourteenth century onwards. Meanwhile, the northern end of the range — which was retained as a single-storey structure — may well have been used for stabling.

Now return to the courtyard to explore the details of the undercrofts.

The Undercrofts

In general terms, the entire layout seen in the principal palace accommodation on the first floor is duplicated in the undercrofts below. All of these undercrofts have highly impressive pitched-stone vaults, a characteristic feature which was by no means unusual in medieval south-west Wales. Writing as early as 1603, the Pembrokeshire historian George Owen (d. 1613) observed:

'The masons were so skillful in old tyme that in these counties most Castells and houses of any accompt were builded with vaultes verye stronglye and substanciallye wrought'

Indeed, although it was abandoned in other areas of Wales (as well as England) from the late thirteenth century onwards, the south-west was unusual in retaining the arrangement of first-floor accommodation over vaulted undercrofts right through the Middle Ages. There is no doubt that undercrofts would have provided almost temperature-controlled storerooms, useful for both perishable food and drink, and they might also be used for the secure storage of valuable goods. They allowed, too, for easy access to the floor above, avoiding the long corridors and covered passageways which are a feature of many other medieval great houses.

Superficially, the undercrofts at the bishop's palace are all very similar; however, close observation allows us to suggest a variety of functions carried out in different areas. Some of the windows, for example, were glazed whereas those in other units were not. In some cases there was direct access from the undercroft to an independent latrine, or perhaps to the first floor. And finally we may note whether or not the doors could be locked.

You may care to explore the various chambers at will, though it may be helpful to highlight some of the more significant details, beginning in the east range at the bishop's chapel and working back around the courtyard to the west range.

We know that the undercroft beneath the bishop's chapel [1] was converted to serve as a squatters' cottage during the eighteenth century. A fireplace was created at the far end and a window was punched through the precinct wall. A narrow staircase within the thickness of the wall rises up to a latrine, perilously perched between the chapel and the palace gatehouse.

The undercrofts beneath the bishop's solar [2] are set out in a T-shaped plan. As you enter from the courtyard, the room to the right gave access to the dais end of the bishop's hall. The room to the left had access to the bishop's solar and also to its own latrine. The long undercroft beneath the east wing provided a secure store, but it contains the walled-in cesspit from the latrine above.

Next you will find a pair of undercrofts in the east range below the bishop's hall [3]. There was access up to the service end of the range.

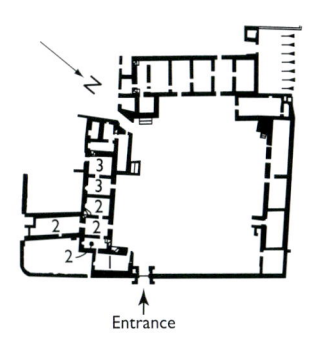

The long barrel-vaulted undercrofts inserted into the west range during the fourteenth century. One of the undercrofts contained the palace well.

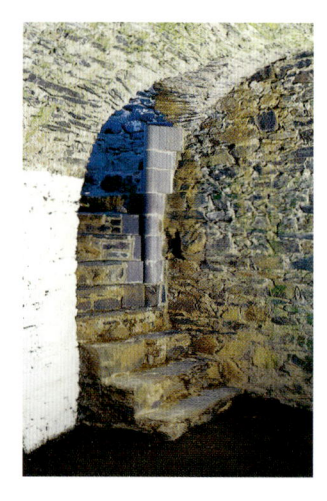

TOUR: THE EXTERIOR OF THE PALACE

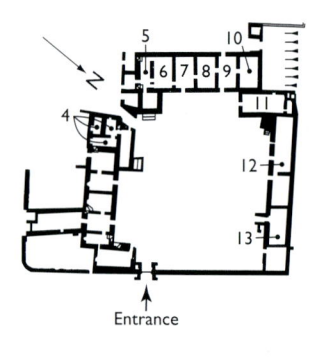

Only two of the three vaulted spaces underneath the kitchen appear to have been accessible [4]. From these there was direct access to the kitchen itself and they may well have served as the principal food store.

In the south range, a very impressive group of six undercrofts was laid out to serve the great hall above. The narrow bay at the eastern end [5] is situated at the foot of the two staircases down from the service end of the hall (p. 37). Rather like the arrangement seen in a modern restaurant, one stair was for movement upwards, the other for down. This first bay was probably the scullery, where dirty dishes might be left.

When you move into the second bay [6], notice that the three windows were glazed. This was the buttery, where wine and beer were poured into flagons and jugs to be carried upstairs. The next two undercrofts [7, 8] were probably used for cellarage, and it was here that the wine and beer were stored in barrels. Beyond, at the western end, one undercroft provided a passage through the range [9], whereas the furthest bay (now housing an exhibition) was a lockable storeroom [10].

The undercroft below the great chapel was a large and well-lit chamber [11], with access to a latrine at the inner end. It was probably designed as quarters for a servant, though it was later to become a cottage for squatters.

Finally, in the west range, where the vaults were a later insertion, there are two long undercrofts [12, 13]. One of these contained the palace well.

The Exterior of the Palace

Before you leave, you may care to walk through the skew passageway in the south-east corner of the courtyard. On the lawns at the other side you can look back on the full splendour of the east range façade, and on the east gable of the great hall with its striking wheel window. For the many pilgrims who entered the cathedral close through its main gate, Porth y Tŵr (pp. 48–49), these were the most prominent elevations of the magnificent palace created by Henry de Gower. Here the arcaded parapet was treated with great richness. The chequerboard work includes panels of white quartz pebbles; there are carved corbels at two levels, and tablet flowers decorate the arches. Notice too that the chequerboard design was applied to the turrets on each of the angles on this side.

Steps leading down to one of the six undercrofts below the great hall and great chamber. Differences between each undercroft indicate that they had separate purposes, ranging from a scullery at the east end to a lockable storeroom at the western limit of the building.

Left: Bishop Henry sought to impose unity on the palace as a whole by using a range of decorative devices, perhaps nowhere better displayed than in the distinctive arcaded parapet shown here, on the east range. It is this view which no doubt impressed medieval visitors to the palace, as indeed it does their counterparts today.

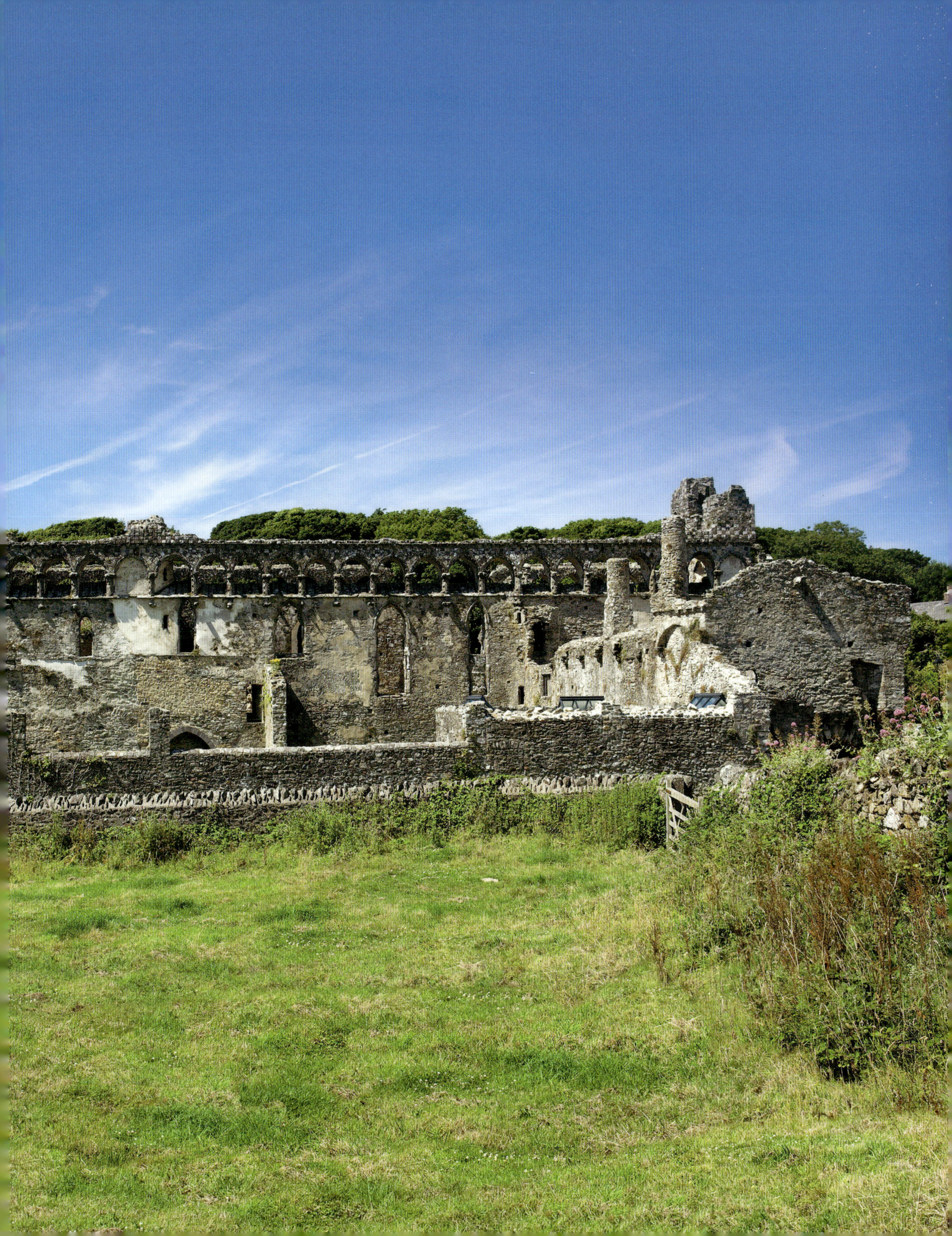

TOUR: THE EXTERIOR OF THE PALACE

Just below the arcade and the wheel window on the gable end of the great hall, there are two roof lines. These represent different phases of the passageway linking the hall with the kitchen.

In the exterior face of the east range, you will see that there is a complex junction between the bishop's hall and the later kitchen. In fact, it incorporates two arches and a wall from the original kitchen. Notice the very clear outfall of the kitchen floor drain (p. 31). However, the function of the three arched recesses within the wall below the bishop's hall is uncertain. The stubs of walls projecting forward are of relatively modern date.

To complete your tour, continue around to the exterior of the southern range. Of far less prominence in the medieval complex, the elevations on this side were treated in a much plainer fashion.

The exterior of the east gable of the great hall and the southern end of the east range. Two roof lines below the wheel window mark the different phases of the passageway linking the kitchen with the hall.

The Cathedral Close

The cathedral close at St Davids covered an area of some 16 acres (6.5ha) and was enclosed within a battlemented stone wall about 1,200 yards (1,100m) long. The close was entered by one of four gates: Porth y Tŵr (Tower Gate), Porth Padrig (Patrick's Gate), Porth Boning (Boning's Gate) and Porth Gwyn (White Gate). Though the plans and positions of all these gates are shown on Joseph Lord's map of 1720 (p. 11), the only one to survive is Porth y Tŵr, which led from the town into the close. The sites of the other three gateways are marked by the points where roads still enter the former boundaries of the close. Porth y Tŵr was itself built against an earlier freestanding octagonal tower (now the cathedral belfry). It was equipped with a portcullis and a double gate within the passage, and a separate pedestrian access was also incorporated. The room alongside the passage served as the bishop's prison and contains a bottle dungeon. The hall and chamber above were used by the medieval town council and mayor.

In all, the battlemented wall and its four gateways gave a defensive feel to the close. Indeed, an anonymous sixteenth-century antiquary considered that, 'when well look'd to', they could have defended the canons 'against a whole Country that should have come against them with Spears and Shields'. But in fact the walls are far too long to be defended successfully against a determined attack. Their purpose was much more likely one of controlling the movement of pilgrims and townspeople into the close during the day, and of securing the cathedral and canons' houses against intruders and vagabonds at night.

We cannot be certain just which of the medieval bishops laid out the formal arrangements in the close, or built the walls and gates. However, Thomas Bek (1280–93) was certainly responsible for reorganizing the cathedral chapter and instructed the canons to enclose their houses in 1287 (p. 11). And in

1344 it was Henry de Gower (1328–47) who enforced the canons to reside at St Davids, requiring each to provide himself with a house fit to live in within 'the new close' (p. 15). In fact, his successor, Bishop Fastolfe (1353–61), credited Gower with laying out the close, but Bishop Houghton (1362–89) complained that the gates and walls were in ruins, and to a great extent 'consumed with age'.

The best surviving sections of the close wall run north-west from the site of Porth Padrig, where the battlemented wall with its wall-walk behind stands over 13 feet (4m) high. In the valley bottom, a small square tower contained a sluice to control the water in the mill leat running beneath. On the opposite bank of the river, where the wall runs up the hill, the gable ends of two earlier buildings are incorporated within its masonry. Beyond, there is clear evidence that the wall was extended up the hill to a circular dovecote belonging to the bishop's palace.

Within the bounds of the close, the land was divided into a number of smaller walled precincts. The eastern quadrant housed the cathedral and cemetery, St Mary's College (founded in 1377) and the Vicars' College. The western quadrant was devoted to the bishop's palace with its gardens and orchards. And the northern and southern quadrants contained the houses and grounds of the various canons of the cathedral chapter. Most of these buildings survived to be mapped in 1720.

In the later Middle Ages, the close would have looked very different from the rather empty, and in parts wild, place that we see today. In addition to the bishop's palace, there were nine other major houses within their own walled and gated precincts, each with a neat individual garden and orchard. The two colleges would have had large domestic quarters with their members moving to and from their chapels, and also to the cathedral to celebrate the many daily services. Now only parts of the deanery and the treasurer's house retain any of their medieval core. There is also one ruinous wall of the archdeacon of Cardigan's house standing alongside the road to Porth Boning. These few fragments remind us what has been lost or rebuilt in the last 300 years.

The close wall surrounding the cathedral and bishop's palace probably dates from the end of the thirteenth century. The south-west segment is one of the better-preserved stretches.

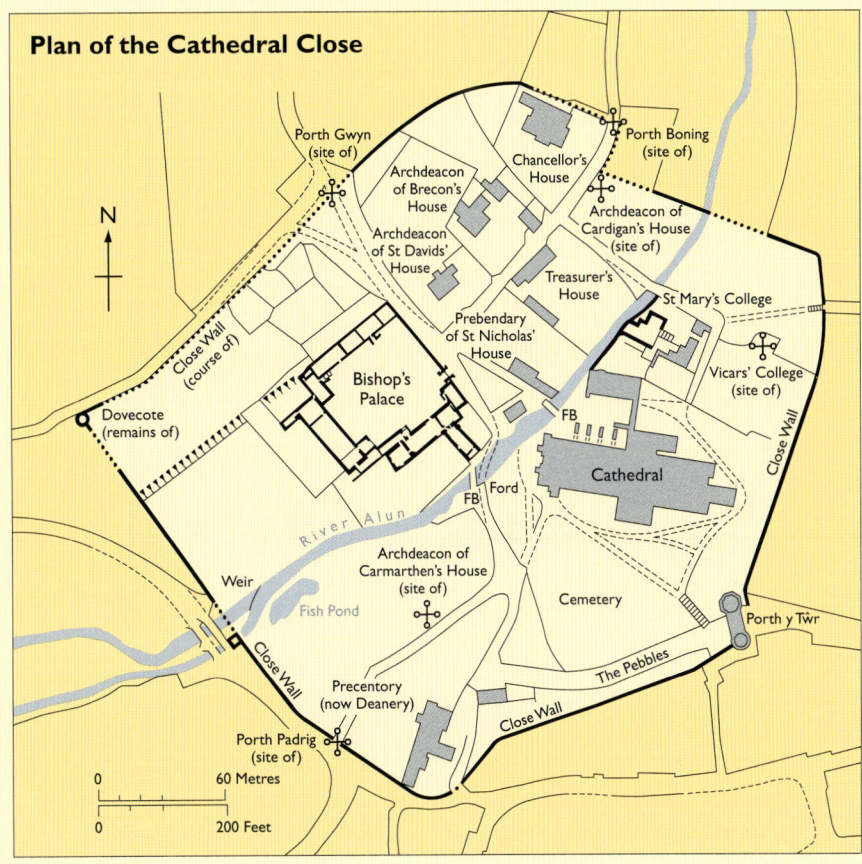

Plan of the Cathedral Close

St Non's Chapel

The site traditionally identified as the chapel of Blessed Non, mother of St David, is located in the centre of a field above St Non's Bay. The remains offer no clue as to its date, nor of its function, since no architectural detail survives. Unlike the majority of Christian buildings, the structure is aligned north and south, probably due to the steep fall in the ground, a fact which may explain the massive masonry at its southern end. This is probably a platform on which the building was constructed rather than the remains of an earlier building, as has been suggested. On the other hand, the site has undergone considerable vicissitudes since the medieval period, when it was reckoned as the 'chief and principal' of the many pilgrimage chapels scattered around the parish of St Davids.

After the chapel passed out of use at the Reformation, it appears to have been converted into a dwelling-house, which was itself in ruins by the mid-nineteenth century. In the late sixteenth century, the site was a leek garden; in the last century the remains of the chapel were piled with stones gathered from the surrounding field. This was a far cry from its heyday in the early sixteenth century when offerings from it and the other pilgrimage chapels were brought every Saturday to the cathedral chapter house and divided among the canons 'by the dishful'. It was conserved in the 1950s, and is now maintained by Cadw.

Although the first reference to the chapel is in 1335, a tradition of considerable antiquity has designated this spot on the cliffs as the birthplace of St David. The earliest *vita* (life) of the saint written about 1090 by Rhigyfarch does not, however, specify the exact location of that event. An early date for the site can be suggested from the 'stone coffins' found during digging for earth within the building in the early nineteenth century. These may perhaps be slab-lined graves of the early medieval period. Resting against the south-east corner of the chapel is a rough pillar cross marked with a simple, incised, linear Latin ring-cross, dating possibly from the seventh or eighth century. Although it was once built into the walls, there is no certainty that it had any direct connection with the chapel.

Finds of a later period included a 'curious pottery image of a head and shoulders' filled with a 'prodigious hard cement'. A fine half brass of a priest, dating perhaps from the fifteenth century also came from the site. Both of these are now lost.

As was so often the case in medieval Wales, the chapel is associated with a well, which lies to the east, below the modern retreat house and chapel. In the late sixteenth century the well was covered with a stone roof, with benches around the walls. Its popularity as a wishing well, and the use of its waters to cure various complaints and to dip babies in, continued into the eighteenth century when repairs were made to the structure. In its present form it dates from 1951, when the Roman Catholic church restored it.

A fine half brass of a priest, dating from perhaps the fifteenth century, is known to have come from the site, but is now lost.

Left: This rough pillar cross, which dates possibly from the seventh or eighth century, now stands in the south-east corner of the chapel.

Opposite: St Non's Chapel — traditionally the birthplace of St David — lies isolated in a field overlooking St Non's Bay. It was undoubtedly a significant place of pilgrimage during the Middle Ages.

The chapel, as was so often the case in medieval Wales, was associated with a holy well. The current arrangement above the well head dates from a restoration in 1951.

Non, the saint to whom both chapel and well are dedicated, is traditionally said to be the mother of St David. The Latin 'life' refers to her as Nonnita (a diminutive form of Non), who was violated by a certain Sanctus, a king of Ceredigion, and in due course gave birth to the patron saint. It also tells us that the church was later erected on the spot. Built into the altar of this church, we are told there was a stone bearing the impression made by Nonnita's fingers during the pains of birth. This may have been a stone inscribed with ogam characters — an Old Irish alphabet — but no trace of it survives today.

Churches and chapels dedicated to Non frequently appear near those dedicated to David in Wales, as well as in Cornwall and Brittany. The name Nonnita survived in Welsh as Nynnid, which is regarded as that of a male saint. It may be that its similarity to the word 'nun' led to confusion between the name of a male companion of David and his mother, and to the invention or adaptation of the unedifying story of the circumstances of his conception and birth. Similar stories are told of other Welsh saints.

Further Reading

Julia Barrow, editor, *St Davids Episcopal Acta 1085–1280* (Cardiff 1998).

A. D. R. Caröe, 'Porth-y-Twr, St David's', *Archaeologia Cambrensis* **103** (1954), 1–17.

Nicola Coldstream, *The Decorated Style: Architecture and Ornament 1240–1360* (London 1994).

N. Edwards, *A Corpus of Early Medieval Inscribed Stones and Stone Sculpture in Wales, Volume II, South-West Wales* (Cardiff 2007), 449–50.

J. W. Evans, *St Non's Chapel, St Davids, Dyfed* (HMSO, Cardiff 1976).

Wyn Evans and Roger Worsley, *St. Davids Cathedral 1181–1981* (St Davids 1981).

J. Wyn Evans and J. M. Wooding, editors, *St David of Wales: Cult, Church and Nation* (Woodbridge 2007).

Francis Green, editor, *Menevia Sacra* by Edward Yardley (Cambrian Archaeological Association, London 1927).

R. F. Isaacson, editor, and R. Arthur Roberts, *The Episcopal Registers of St. David's 1397 to 1518*, 3 volumes, Cymmrodorion Record Series 6 (London 1917–20).

Heather James, 'The Cult of St David in the Middle Ages', in Martin Carver, editor, *In Search of Cult* (Woodbridge 1993), 105–12.

J. W. James, editor, *Rhigyfarch's Life of St. David* (Cardiff 1967).

Thomas Beaumont James, *The Palaces of Medieval England c. 1050–1550* (London 1990).

Francis Jones, *The Holy Wells of Wales* (Cardiff 1954); reprinted in paperback (Cardiff 1992).

Francis Jones, 'Medieval Records Relating to the Diocese of St Davids', *Journal of the Historical Society of the Church in Wales* **14** (1964), 9–24.

William Basil Jones and Edward Augustus Freeman, *The History and Antiquities of St. David's* (London and Tenby 1856); reprinted (Haverfordwest 1998).

Thomas Lloyd, Julian Orbach and Robert Scourfield, *The Buildings of Wales: Pembrokeshire* (London 2004).

C. A. Ralegh Radford, *The Bishop's Palace St David's*, (HMSO, London 1934); second edition (HMSO, London 1953).

P. A. Robson, *The Cathedral Church of St David's* (London 1901).

Michael Thompson, *Medieval Bishops' Houses in England and Wales* (Aldershot 1998).

Rick Turner, with Nicola Coldstream, Veronica Evans, John Godbert and Bevis Sale, 'St Davids Bishop's Palace', *The Antiquaries Journal* **80** (2000), 87–194.

Glanmor Williams, *The Welsh Church from Conquest to Reformation*, second edition (Cardiff 1976).

Glanmor Williams 'Henry de Gower (?1278–1347): Bishop and Builder', *Archaeologia Cambrensis* **130** (1981), 1–18.

Browne Willis, *A Survey of the Cathedral Church of St. David's* (London 1717).